# CHILDREN'S
## QUICK
## & EASY
# COOK
# BOOK

# CHILDREN'S
## QUICK
## & EASY
# COOK BOOK

### ANGELA WILKES

**DK**

# CONTENTS

## DELIGHTFUL DESSERTS

# NOTE FOR ADULTS

You will need to supervise children AT ALL TIMES when making a recipe. Make sure to complete the steps that require sharp knives, other potentially dangerous equipment, or a heat source to make a recipe.

##  KITCHEN SAFETY

- When you see the warning triangle, take extra care.
- Be careful around hot ovens and gas or electric stovetops, making sure you know whether the oven or stovetop is on and protecting your hands when touching or lifting anything hot from, or onto, or into it. Oven mitts are your friends here!
- Take extra care when handling hot liquids or hot pans, being careful to avoid spills and protecting your hands (with oven mitts or a dish towel) when moving or holding them. Tell an adult immediately if you get a burn.
- When using power tools, such as food processors and mixers, check if they're on, and don't put your hands near the moving parts until you have switched them off at the socket.
- Carefully follow the temperature instructions for preheating the oven in each recipe.

## WEIGHTS AND MEASUREMENTS

Carefully measure the ingredients before you start a recipe. Use measuring spoons, kitchen scales, and a measuring cup, as necessary. Spoon measures should always be level. Below are the abbreviations and full names for the measurements used in this book:

**METRIC**
g = gram
kg = kilogram
ml = milliliter
cm = centimeter

**US MEASURES**
oz = ounce

lb = pound
fl oz = fluid ounce
in = inch

**SPOON MEASURES**
tsp = teaspoon
tbsp = tablespoon

## ⅄❢ HOW MANY?

This lists the amount of portions a recipe makes. Remember to be treat-wise and don't go overboard by eating more than one portion.

## INGREDIENTS

Make sure you have all your ingredients laid out before you start to make a recipe. You'll probably have most ingredients in your kitchen already, but some you will need to buy.
- Always use the type of flour specified in a recipe—all-purpose, bread, or self-rising.
- Use Grade A, large, free-range eggs unless otherwise stated.
- For recipes that require milk, you can use whole, low-fat, or skim milk.

## BE ALLERGY AWARE!

Always check that the ingredients for a recipe do not contain anything that you or anyone eating the food may be allergic to or that are not part of your recommended diet. Wash all dishes well after using an allergen like peanut butter.

## GLOSSARY AND SPECIAL EQUIPMENT

Refer to the glossary of methods on pages 90–93. Buy or borrow any special equipment before making a recipe.

## KITCHEN HYGIENE

Please note that when you're in the kitchen, you need to follow these important rules to keep germs in check.
- Always wash your hands before you start any recipe.
- Use hot, soapy water to clean cutting boards after each use.
- Keep your cooking area clean and have a cloth handy to mop up any spills.
- Always check the use-by date on all ingredients.
- Wash your hands after handling raw eggs and raw meat.

##  HOW LONG?

This tells you how many minutes and hours a recipe will take to prepare, bake, chill, or freeze. Remember though that preparation times might be a little longer if it's the first time you're making a recipe.

# SUPERFAST SNACKS

## EQUIPMENT

- Cutting board
- Bread knife • Baking sheet
- Knife • Spoon

## INGREDIENTS

- 1 or 2 bagels per person

### SUGGESTED FILLINGS

- Cream cheese
- Smoked salmon
- Peanut butter
- Banana, sliced
- Hummus
- Carrot, grated
- Cucumber, sliced

Smoked salmon and cream cheese filling, on a seeded bagel.

Peanut butter and banana filling, on a plain bagel.

*Replace smoked salmon with ham, if you prefer.*

Banana slices

Peanut butter

Hummus, cucumber, and carrot filling on an everthing bagel.

# BAGEL BONANZA

Get creative with these sweet and savory fillings. Gently toasted, the soft, warm bagels are so satisfying and delicious.

**1** Cut the bagels in half and place on a baking sheet, cut-side up. Heat the broiler and toast the bagels until the edges are golden.

**2** Layer the bottoms with the filling of your choice, then put the tops on the bagels and eat them while they're still warm.

Crème
fraîche

# CROISSANT FEAST

This pastry is usually eaten for breakfast, but here it gets a makeover—and with different fillings, it is perfect for any time of day!

## EQUIPMENT

- Cutting board
- Baking sheet • Bread knife
- Knife • Grater

## INGREDIENTS

- 1 or 2 croissants per person

### SUGGESTED FILLINGS

- Crème fraîche
- Strawberry jam
- Dark chocolate
- Sliced ham
- Grated Cheddar cheese

⚠ **1** Preheat the oven to 350°F (180°C). Place the croissants on a baking sheet. Warm the croissants, cut them in half, then add the filling of your choice.

This croissant was made by spreading the bottom with a layer of crème fraîche and topping it with strawberry jam.

Make this savory croissant by laying a slice of ham on the bottom, sprinkling grated cheese on top, and toasting it for a minute (or until melted) before adding the top half.

Try different kinds of jam or use stewed apple or fruit compote instead.

This sweet treat is so easy—just sprinkle grated dark chocolate onto the cut sides of the croissant and let it melt.

11

## EQUIPMENT

- Cutting board
- Bread knife • Baking sheet
- Sharp knife • Small bowl
- Pastry brush

## INGREDIENTS

- 1 baguette/French bread loaf
- 1 garlic clove
- Olive oil, for brushing

### SUGGESTED TOPPINGS

- Tomato sauce
- Mozzarella cheese, sliced
- Tomatoes, sliced
- Hummus
- Pitted black olives, sliced
- Parsley
- Green pesto
- Cherry tomatoes, sliced
- Canned tuna fish
- Celery, chopped
- Fresh chives, chopped
- Sliced ham
- Cream cheese
- Sliced salami

# CRUNCHY CROSTINI

These toasted slices of baguette make for a fresh snack or party food, and they're a great way to experiment with new flavor combinations.

**1** Preheat the broiler. Carefully cut the baguette into slices, then toast the pieces of bread on both sides until golden brown.

**2** Cut the garlic clove in half. Rub one side of each piece of toast with the garlic, brush it with olive oil, and add the topping of your choice.

**Mozzarella and ham**

**Green pesto and cherry tomatoes**

**Cream cheese with salami**

**Tuna topped with celery and chopped chives**

**Tomato sauce, mozzarella, and sliced tomato**

**Hummus and olives**

## EQUIPMENT

- Cutting board • Knife
- Spoon • Bread knife
- Toothpicks, for presentation only

## INGREDIENTS

- 3 slices bread

### FOR THE SPICY ONE

- Butter
- Chicken, cooked, cooled, and sliced
- Diced cucumber and chopped mint in plain yogurt
- Mango chutney

### FOR THE TRICOLOR ONE

- Mozzarella cheese, sliced
- Tomato, sliced
- Avocado, pitted and sliced
- French dressing

### FOR THE FESTIVE ONE

- Sausage, cooked, cooled, and sliced
- Mayonnaise
- Turkey, cooked, cooled, and sliced
- Cranberry sauce
- Lettuce (optional)

Brown bread is used to make this tangy chicken and chutney club.

The tricolor club sandwich gets its name from its three bright colors: red, white, and green.

**Toothpicks**

To make this festive club sandwich, spread the bread with mayonnaise. Lettuce can be added for extra freshness, color, and crunch.

# DOUBLE-DECKER CLUB SANDWICH

Add another slice of bread to your regular sandwich and you can double up on your chosen filling! Secure it all with a toothpick, but remove it before tucking in.

**1** If your sandwich has butter or mayonnaise on it, spread it over the bread. Layer half the ingredients over one slice. Add the second slice of bread, then another layer of ingredients.

**2** Add the third slice, then cut the sandwich in quarters. For presentation, pop a toothpick in to hold everything together, but remove it before eating the sandwiches

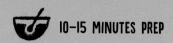

## EQUIPMENT

- Large saucepan with lid
- Small saucepan
- Wooden spoon

## INGREDIENTS

- 2 tbsp vegetable oil
- ⅓ cup (55 g) popping corn

### FOR MAPLE PEANUT POPS

- 2 tbsp butter
- ¼ cup (45 g) crunchy peanut butter
- 1 tbsp maple syrup

### FOR CHEESY POPS

- 2 tbsp butter
- ¼ cup (30 g) grated Parmesan cheese
- ½ tsp salt

Cheesy popcorn

Maple syrup

# POPCORN TREATS

This fun, puffed-corn movie treat is ready in just a few minutes. Choose which flavor you'd like to try, or go for both! You'll need to eat the popcorn as soon as you make it.

Maple peanut pops

## Popping the corn

**1** Heat the vegetable oil in the large saucepan until hot. Add the popping corn, spreading it out to cover the bottom of the pan.

**2** Cook the corn until it sstarts to pop, then put on the lid. Cook it for 2–3 more minutes, while carefully shaking the pan. When all the corn has popped, carefully remove the lid and pour the popcorn into a bowl.

## Maple peanut pops

**1** Melt the butter, peanut butter, and maple syrup in the small saucepan over low heat. Stir it well, then pour it over the popcorn and mix well.

## Cheesy pops

**1** Melt the butter in a small saucepan over low heat. Stir in the grated cheese and salt. Spoon the mixture over the popcorn. Mix well.

## EQUIPMENT

- Small kitchen brush
- Cutting board
- Sharp knife • Small bowl
- Pastry brush
- Baking sheet

## INGREDIENTS

- 1 lb (450 g) Russet potatoes
- 4–5 tbsp sunflower or olive oil
- Salt and freshly ground black pepper

# POTATO WEDGES

By keeping the skin on these potato wedges you get an extra bit of fiber. This recipe works well with sweet potatoes, too.

To give the wedges a Mediterranean flavor, sprinkle them with dried, mixed herbs once baked.

**1** Preheat the oven to 475°F (240°C). Cut the potatoes in half lengthwise, then cut them into thin wedges.

**2** Brush the baking sheet with oil. Lay the potato wedges in one layer on top, then brush them with oil and season.

**3** Bake the potato wedges on the top rack of the oven for 20–25 minutes, or until crisp, golden brown, and puffy, turning them once so they brown evenly.

Ketchup

## Parsnip wedges

Make delicious parsnip wedges by baking parsnips in the same way as the potatoes.

Chunky wedges go well with many dishes and make a tasty snack on their own.

10 MINUTES PREP FOR EACH OPTION

SERVES 4

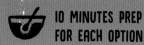

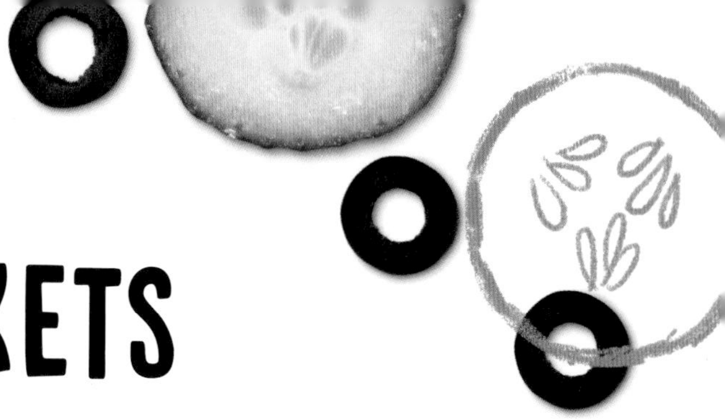

# PITA POCKETS

These stuffed pita pockets are a great way to try lots of different textures in one mouthful. Go for something creamy and something crunchy!

## EQUIPMENT

- Cutting board
- Sharp knife
- Baking sheet
- Spoon

## INGREDIENTS

- 1 or 2 pita bread rounds per person

### SUGGESTED FILLINGS

- Guacamole
- Sliced, cold, cooked chicken
- Sliced tomato
- Hummus
- Sliced red bell pepper
- Sliced cucumber
- Sliced pitted black olives
- Shredded lettuce
- Turkish-style lamb (see page 32)
- Yogurt
- Fresh mint leaves

**1** Prepare the ingredients for the filling of your choice. Preheat the broiler.

**2** Heat the pita rounds under the broiler for 1 minute on each side, then slit them open and add the filling.

To make this pocket, fill it with guacamole and chicken. Tomato can be added for extra color.

The filling in this pocket is shredded lettuce, meatballs, and a dollop of yogurt mixed with fresh mint.

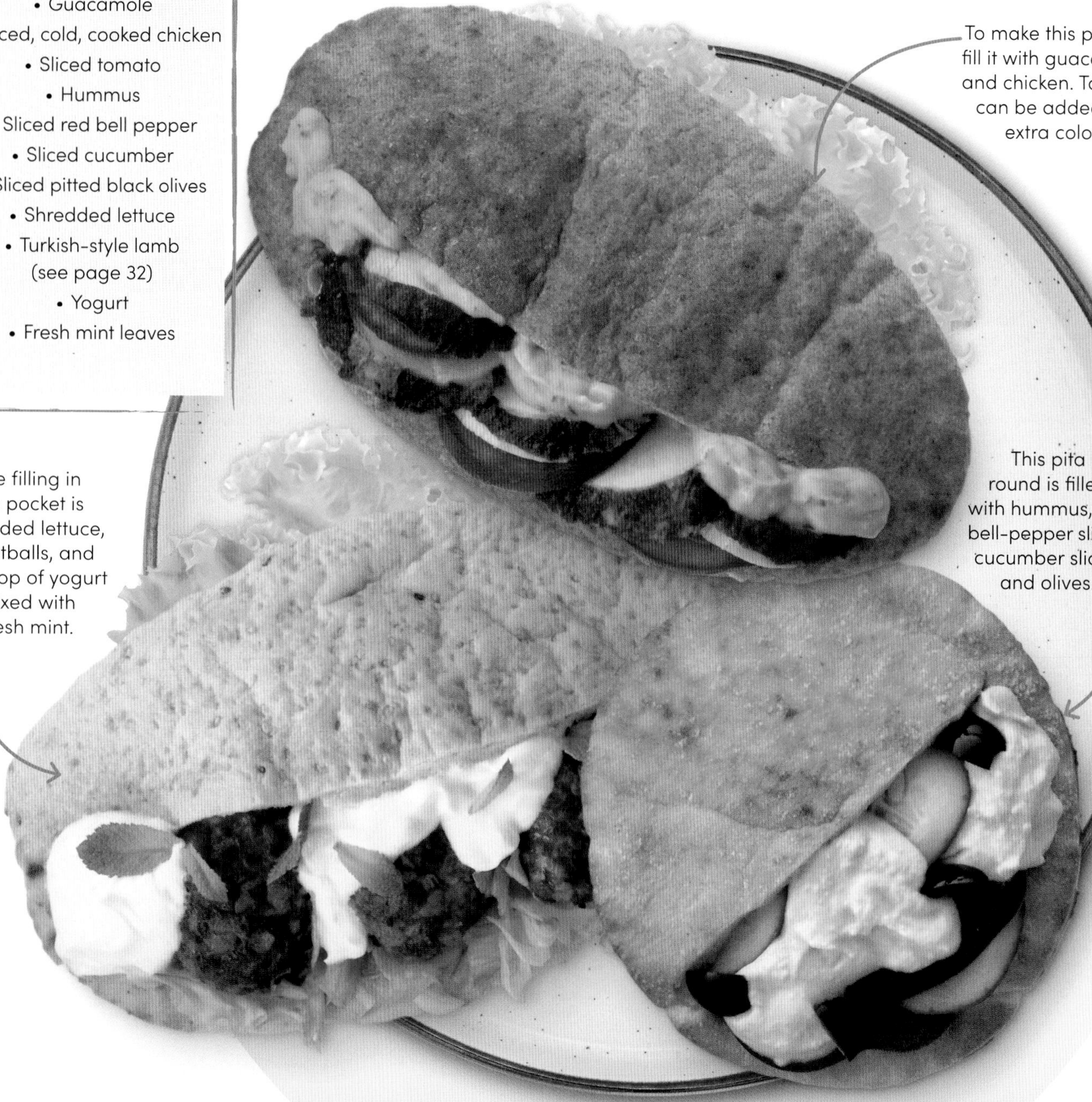

This pita round is filled with hummus, red bell-pepper slices, cucumber slices, and olives.

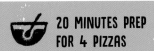
## EQUIPMENT

- Cutting board
- Baking sheet • Bread knife
- Spoon

## INGREDIENTS

- 1 English muffin per person
- Pizza or pasta sauce

### SUGGESTED TOPPINGS

- Grated mozzarella cheese
- Cherry tomatoes, halved
- Fresh basil leaves
- Strips of ham
- Canned chopped pineapple
- Sliced pepperoni
- Red bell pepper, diced
- Green bell pepper, diced

Top a margherita-style pizza with cherry tomatoes and fresh basil leaves.

Not everyone likes Hawaiian pizza, but if you're a fan of the meat and fruit combo, this one's for you.

# CHEAT'S PIZZA

This quick and easy pizza recipe gives you all those classic pizza flavors in no time! Use pitas instead of muffins, if you like.

⚠️ **1** Preheat the broiler. Slice the muffins in half with a bread knife. Toast the muffins for 1 to 2 minutes on each side.

**2** Put a spoonful of pizza or pasta sauce on each toasted muffin, then spread it out evenly.

⚠️ **3** Layer on the toppings you like best, then broil the pizzas for a few more minutes, until the cheese is melted and bubbly.

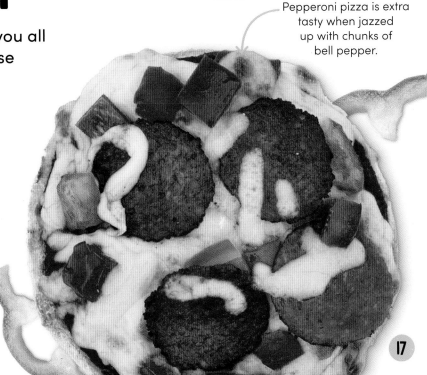

Pepperoni pizza is extra tasty when jazzed up with chunks of bell pepper.

## EQUIPMENT

- Large saucepan
- Colander
- Cutting board
- Bread knife • Sharp knife
- Spoon • Bowl • Lemon squeezer • Food processor
- Small serving bowl

# HOTDOGS WITH RELISH

Try a soft bun and juicy hotdog with tangy relish to wake up your taste buds. It's the perfect dish for a picnic or backyard party. Make the relish in advance.

Gherkins

## INGREDIENTS

### FOR THE HOTDOGS

- 4 hotdogs
- 4 hotdog buns

### FOR THE RELISH

- 4 large gherkins, coarsely chopped
- ½ small onion, coarsely chopped
- 1 tsp sugar
- ½ tsp ground cinnamon
- 1 tsp mustard
- 1 tbsp cider vinegar
- Salt and freshly ground black pepper

### Making the hotdogs

1. Heat a large saucepan of water until it simmers, then add the hotdogs. Cook them for 5 minutes, then carefully drain them.

2. Warm the buns in the oven for a few minutes, then split each one down the middle. Put a cooked hotdog in each bun.

### Making the relish

1. Pulse the gherkins and onion in the food processor, until finely chopped. Add all the other ingredients. Pulse until combined. If needed, add a tablespoon of pickled gherkin juice.

2. Leave the relish to stand for 1 hour to allow the flavors to develop.

Have some fun squirting mustard or ketchup in a squiggle on top of the hotdogs.

Serve the relish in a small bowl.

## EQUIPMENT

- Cutting board
- Bread knife
- Shallow plate • Spoon
- Large skillet
- Spatula
- Baking sheet • Knife

## INGREDIENTS

- 4 thick slices of a large French baguette
- ⅓ cup (55 g) all-purpose flour
- Salt and freshly ground black pepper
- 4 flat, skinned, boned fish fillets
- 1 tbsp vegetable oil
- 2 tbsp butter
- Butter, for spreading
- A dash of lemon juice
- Ketchup, to serve
- ½ lemon, cut into wedges, to serve

Serve the fish baguettes with wedges of fresh lemon.

Ketchup

The flour gives the fish a crispy coating.

# FISH BAGUETTES

This fancier version of a fish-stick sandwich is worth the effort. Add lettuce if you like, or use soft buns instead of baguettes: it's your call!

**1** Preheat the broiler. Cut each slice of bread in half. Put the flour on to the shallow plate and season it with salt and pepper.

**2** One at a time, lay each fish fillet in the seasoned flour, turning it over so that it is coated with flour on both sides.

**3** Heat the oil and butter in the skillet over medium-high heat. When they are hot, fry the fish for about 3 minutes on each side.

**4** Warm the bread under the broiler, then butter it. Add a dash of lemon juice on the fish fillets. Sandwich each piece of fish in two slices of bread.

# FRUIT SMOOTHIES

If you don't have strawberries, blend up your favorite fruit for this easy smoothie. Freeze the banana and berries before blending and you'll have instant ice cream instead!

## EQUIPMENT

- Cutting board
- Sharp knife
- Blender or food processor
- 2 glasses

## INGREDIENTS

- 6 oz (175 g) strawberries
- 1 ripe banana
- ½ cup (115 g) plain yogurt
- ⅔ cup (150 ml) almond milk

**1** Cut the stems out of the strawberries (called "hulling"). Peel and slice the banana and put it in the blender or food processor.

**2** Add the strawberries, yogurt, and almond milk. Put the lid on the blender and pulse for 1 minute, until smooth and frothy. Pour into the glasses.

Serve the smoothies with colorful paper straws.

These smoothies are made with strawberries. For other flavors, use raspberries, apricots, or pitted cherries.

Apricots

Banana

Strawberry

## EQUIPMENT

- Tall glass
- Ice-cream scoop or large spoon

## INGREDIENTS

- 2 scoops strawberry or vanilla ice cream
- ¼ cup (75 ml) lemon-lime or strawberry soda
- 1 bottle club soda, fizzy lemonade, or cola

# ICE-CREAM SODAS

A classic summertime treat, these are best enjoyed right away, before the ice cream melts!

**1** Put 2 scoops of strawberry or vanilla ice cream into the tall glass, then pour the strawberry or lemon-lime soda over the top.

**2** Slowly pour enough club soda, lemonade, or cola on top of the ice cream to fill the drinking glass.

Vanilla ice cream

Strawberry soda made with strawberry ice cream, strawberry soda, and club soda.

Lime soda made with vanilla ice cream, lemon-lime soda, and lemonade.

21

2 MINUTES PREP
6 MINUTES COOK

SERVES 1

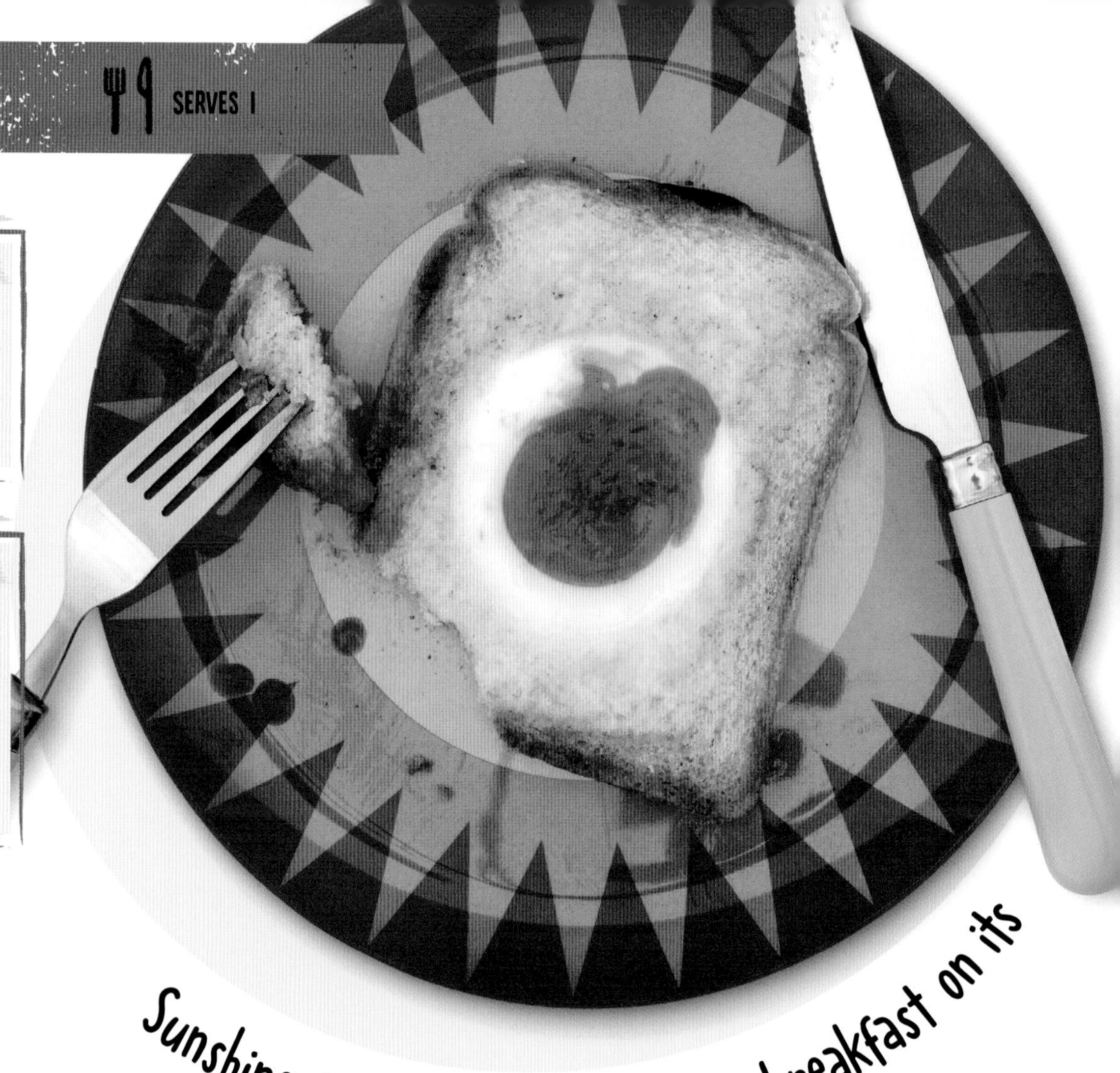

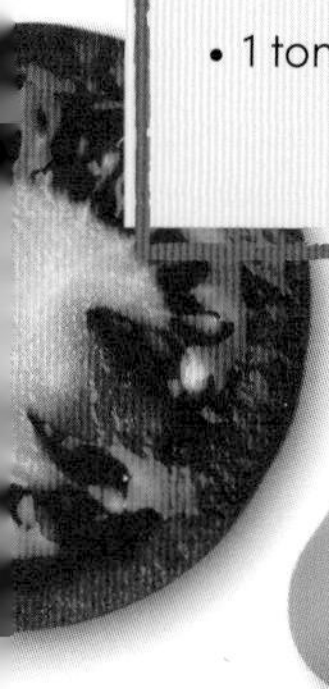

## EQUIPMENT

- Cutting board
- Cookie cutter
- Small bowl
- Skillet
- Spatula

## INGREDIENTS

- 1 slice bread
- 1 egg
- 2 tbsp butter
- 1 tbsp vegetable oil
- 1 tomato, sliced, to serve

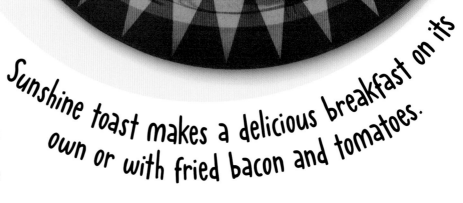

*Sunshine toast makes a delicious breakfast on its own or with fried bacon and tomatoes.*

# SUNSHINE TOAST

Use any shape cookie cutter you like for these egg-in-a-hole toasts—it doesn't need to be round. They're great for brunch, too, served with slices of fresh tomatoes.



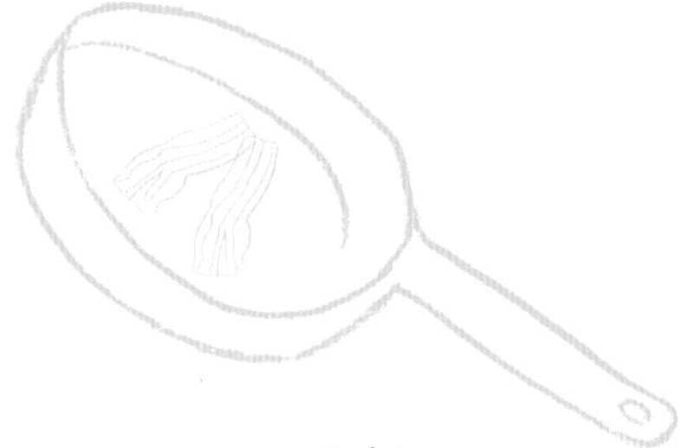

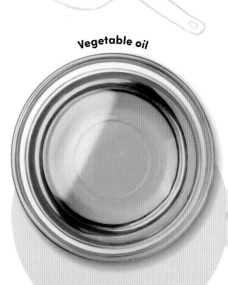

1. Lay the slice of bread down flat and cut a hole in the middle of it with the cookie cutter. Break the egg into the small bowl.
2. Heat the butter and oil in the skillet over medium-high heat. Put the bread in the skillet and fry it on one side for 30 seconds.
3. Turn the slice of bread over with the spatula, then pour the egg out of the bowl and into the hole in the middle of the bread.
4. Fry the bread and egg until the egg white is set but the yolk is still runny. Using the fish slice, lift it out of the pan onto a plate.

Vegetable oil

# SPEEDY MEALS

## EQUIPMENT

- Bowl • Whisk or fork
- Nonstick skillet
- Spatula

# SPEEDY CHEESY OMELET

Cheddar and gruyère are perfect cheeses for this simple, filling egg dish. Fold the omelet, and once you've aced the technique, have fun trying different options. Add the fillings just before you fold the omelet.

## INGREDIENTS

- 2 eggs
- Salt and freshly ground black pepper
- 1 tbsp butter
- 1 tbsp grated cheese
- Chopped fresh parsley for garnish (optional)

**1** Break the eggs into the bowl. Add a little salt and pepper and beat the eggs lightly with a whisk or fork, until frothy.

**2** Melt the butter in the frying pan. When it begins to foam, pour in the beaten eggs, then sprinkle the cheese on top.

**3** As the edges of the omelet set, lift them gently with the spatula and tilt the pan so that the runny egg flows underneath and cooks.

**4** After 1–2 minutes, when the top has set, but is still creamy, loosen the edges of the omelet and fold it in half. Serve right away.

**Omelet made with chopped ham**

**Speedy cheesy omelet**

**Herb omelet flavored with parsley and chives**

## EQUIPMENT

- Saucepan
- Cutting board
- Sharp knife
- Nonstick, ovenproof skillet
- Wooden spoon
- Mixing bowl
- Whisk or fork • Spatula

## INGREDIENTS

- 1 large onion
- 2 medium-sized potatoes
- 1 large red bell pepper
- 2 tbsp sunflower oil
- 4 eggs
- Salt and freshly ground black pepper
- 2 tbsp butter

### Spicy sausage omelet

For a change, you can add other ingredients to the omelet, such as 1 cup (115 g) of cooked spicy sausage cut into chunks.

This omelet is delicious served cold at a picnic.

# SPANISH OMELET

Also known as a tortilla, this hearty egg dish is a great way to use up cooked veggies. Serve it with a garden salad on the side.

**1** Boil the potatoes for 20 minutes. Drain them, then thinly slice. Peel the onion and chop it finely. Cut the bell pepper in half, remove the seeds, and dice it.

**2** Heat the oil in the skillet. Add the onion and bell pepper and cook gently for 5 minutes, until soft. Add the potatoes and cook for 2 minutes more. Set aside.

**3** Beat the eggs in the bowl. Stir in the onion, bell pepper, and potatoes, and season. Melt the butter in the skillet.

**4** Pour the mixture into the skillet and cook over low heat for about 10 minutes, then broil the top under a hot broiler until set and golden.

## EQUIPMENT

- Garlic crusher
- Medium saucepan
- Wooden spoon
- Measuring cup
- Immersion blender

## INGREDIENTS

- 2 tbsp olive oil
- 1 small onion, diced
- 1 clove garlic, crushed
- 15 oz (425 g) can chopped tomatoes
- 2 tbsp tomato paste
- 2 cups (500 ml) hot vegetable stock
- 1 tsp sugar
- Salt and freshly ground black pepper
- Crusty bread, to serve
- 6 fresh basil leaves (optional)

# TOMATO SOUP

This soup is made using canned tomatoes, which are packed with flavor. To make cream of tomato soup, stir in 2 tablespoons of heavy cream when blending.

**1** Heat the olive oil in a medium saucepan over medium-high heat. Add the onion and cook for 5 minutes, until softened but not browned, stirring occasionally.

**2** Add the garlic and cook for 1 minute, then add the chopped tomatoes, tomato paste, stock, and sugar.

**3** Bring to a boil, then cover and simmer for 10 minutes, stirring occasionally. Using an immersion blender, blend until smooth.

**4** Season to taste and serve in bowls, with crusty bread on the side. Garnish with basil leaves, if using.

Use fresh tomatoes for this soup instead of canned tomatoes, if you like. Chop first, before adding them to the pan.

Crusty bread

If you like basil, add some leaves before blending the soup. Use them for garnish, too.

Hearty bread turns
this soup into a
filling meal.

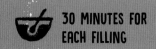
## EQUIPMENT

- Cutting board
- Sharp knife • Garlic press
- Large saucepan
- Skillet • Wooden spoons
- Baking sheet • Spoon
- Mixing bowl • Fork
- Lemon squeezer • Small bowls for toppings

# TACOS AND GUACAMOLE

Have fun filling these crunchy tacos and sprinkling them with colorful toppings, or let everyone help themselves. They are perfect for a celebration (no cutlery needed!).

## INGREDIENTS

### FOR THE MEAT FILLING

- 1 onion
- 1 garlic clove
- 2 tbsp vegetable oil
- 1 lb (450 g) ground beef
- Salt and freshly ground black pepper
- 1 packet taco seasoning

### FOR THE BEAN FILLING

- 1 onion
- 1 carrot
- 1 garlic clove
- 2 tbsp vegetable oil
- Salt and freshly ground black pepper
- Pinch of cayenne pepper
- 1 packet taco seasoning
- 14½ oz (411 g) canned diced tomatoes
- 15 oz (425 g) canned black beans
- ½ tsp hot sauce
- Squeeze of lemon juice

### FOR SERVING

- 16 taco shells
- Salsa • Sour cream
- Shredded lettuce
- Grated cheese
- Cilantro

## Meat filling

**1** Chop the onion and crush the garlic. Heat the oil in a skillet. Add the onion and garlic and cook until soft.

**2** Add the ground beef. Stir it and cook until brown. Season and add the taco seasoning. Cook over low heat for 10 minutes.

## Filling the tacos

**1** Preheat the oven to 350°F (180°C). Place 8 taco shells (for each filling) on the baking sheet. Warm the shells in the oven for 3 minutes.

## Bean filling

**1** Chop the onion, carrot, and garlic. Heat the oil in the saucepan. Add the vegetables and garlic. Cook until soft. Stir in the spices.

**2** Season and stir in the canned tomatoes, beans, hot sauce, and lemon juice. Cook for 15 minutes, or until the sauce has thickened.

**2** Spoon the fillings into the warm taco shells, then add the toppings, such as the shredded lettuce and the grated cheese.

**Sour cream**

## INGREDIENTS

### FOR THE GUACAMOLE

- 1 tomato
- ½ small onion
- 2 large, ripe avocados
- Juice of 2 limes
- ½ tsp hot sauce
- Salt and freshly ground black pepper

**Guacamole**

## ⚠ Making the guacamole

Carefully cut the tomato in half, seed, and chop into small pieces. Finely chop the onion. Cut up the avocado flesh, place it in the bowl, and mash it with a fork to make a smooth, thick paste. Squeeze in the lime juice, then add the hot sauce, salt, and pepper. Add the tomatoes and mix everything together until smooth.

**Salsa**

Bean-filled taco with lettuce and grated cheese

Everyone can pick what they'd like to have in their taco. What's your favorite filling?

## Great party food!

Meat-filled taco with onion, cheese, and lettuce

Vegetarian feast!

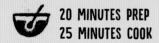

**20 MINUTES PREP**
**25 MINUTES COOK**

**SERVES 4**

## EQUIPMENT

- Cutting board
- Sharp knife • Garlic press
- Skillet • Wooden spoon • Large saucepan
- Colander • Fork
- Grater or food processor
- Baking dish • Paper towels

## INGREDIENTS

- 1 onion
- 1 garlic clove
- 2 tbsp olive oil
- 2 x 14½ oz (411 g) cans diced tomatoes
- 1 tbsp tomato paste
- Salt and freshly ground black pepper
- 9 oz (250 g) rigatoni or penne pasta
- 1 lb (450 g) spicy or sweet Italian sausage
- 1 oz (50 g) Cheddar cheese, about ½ cup grated
- 1 oz (50 g) bread, about ¾ cup bread crumbs

# PERFECT PASTA

You can eat this pasta dish for lunch or dinner. The crunchy, cheesy topping makes this casserole extra special.

**1** Preheat the oven to 425°F (220°C). Peel the onion and chop it finely. Peel the garlic and crush it or chop it finely. Heat the oil in a skillet over medium heat.

**2** Add the onion and garlic to the pan and cook until soft, then add the canned tomatoes and tomato paste and stir well.

**3** Let the pasta sauce simmer over low heat for 10 minutes. Season with salt and pepper. Add the tomato mix to the baking dish.

**4** Boil salted water in the large saucepan. Add the pasta and cook for 12 minutes, until just tender, then drain it in a colander. Add the pasta to the baking dish and toss.

**5** Wipe the skillet. If using whole sausages, prick them with a fork. Cook over medium heat until browned, about 10–12 minutes.

**6** Drain the sausage meat on paper towels, and, once cool, cut any whole sausages into chunky slices.

When the pasta is baked, the cheese melts into the bread crumbs, forming a crisp, golden topping.

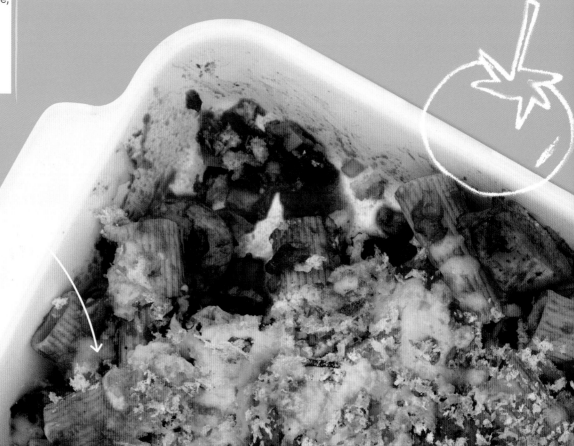

Baked pasta is delicious and very filling, so a simple green salad is all you need to serve with it.

⚠ **7** Grate the cheese for the topping. Grate the bread into bread crumbs or make the bread crumbs in a food processor.

**8** Stir the cooked sausage into the tomato and pasta mixture in the baking dish.

⚠ **9** Sprinkle the bread crumbs and grated cheese over the pasta. Bake for 20–25 minutes, until the topping is crisp.

If you are cooking for vegetarians, omit the sausages and increase the amount of cheese used in the topping to 3 oz (85 g), about 1¼ cups grated.

You can vary this recipe by using different pasta shapes. Check the cooking time on the package, as it may differ depending on which type of pasta you're using.

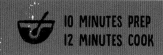
## EQUIPMENT

- Cutting board
- Sharp knife
- Garlic press • Mixing bowl
- Wooden spoon
- Bamboo skewers
- Small bowl • Pastry brush
- Grill pan

Lemon wedges can be squeezed over the kebabs.

## INGREDIENTS

- 1 small onion
- 1 garlic clove
- 1 lb (450 g) ground lamb
- A few fresh mint leaves
- 1 tsp ground allspice
- 1 tsp ground cinnamon
- Salt and freshly ground black pepper
- Vegetable oil, for grilling
- Lemon wedges, to serve
- Shredded lettuce, to serve
- Pita bread, to serve

# TURKISH KEBABS

Serve these tender and juicy, Turkish-style lamb kebabs with shredded lettuce and toasted pitas. For variety, mold them into balls instead of sausage shapes, if you like!

**1** Peel the onion and chop it finely. Peel and crush the garlic. Put the onion, garlic, and ground lamb in the mixing bowl.

**2** Finely chop the mint. Sprinkle the mint, allspice, and cinnamon over the lamb, season with salt and pepper, and mix to form a paste.

**3** Split the mixture into 8 portions and mold them into sausage shapes around the skewers. Brush them with oil.

**4** Heat a grill pan over high heat. Cook the kebabs for 10–12 minutes, turning them until they are brown all over and cooked through.

Vegetable oil

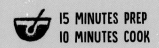
## EQUIPMENT

- Cutting board
- Sharp knife • Dish towel
- Garlic press • Colander
- Large bowl • Fork or food processor • Wooden spoon
- Skillet • Spatula
- Paper towels

## INGREDIENTS

- 1 medium onion
- 2 tbsp chopped flat-leaf parsley
- 2 garlic cloves
- 2 x 15oz (425g) cans chickpeas
- 2 tbsp all-purpose flour
- 1 tsp ground coriander
- 1 tsp ground cumin
- Freshly ground black pepper
- Vegetable oil, for frying
- Pita bread, to serve
- Plain yogurt, to serve
- Cucumber, sliced
- Red onion, sliced
- Tomato, sliced
- Cayenne pepper, to serve

# FALAFEL

Made with chickpeas, these patties are fluffy inside, with a crunchy coating. Great as finger food or stuffed into pita bread.

**1** Finely chop the onion. Wash, dry, and chop the parsley. Peel and crush the garlic and rinse and drain the chickpeas.

**2** Mash the chickpeas in the food processor or in the large bowl using the fork. Mix in the onion, garlic, flour, parsley, coriander, and cumin. Season with the pepper.

**3** With floured hands, roll the mixture into 8 balls, each about the size of golf balls, then flatten them to make small patties.

**4** Heat the oil in the skillet over medim-high heat. Fry the falafel for a few minutes on each side, until golden brown. Drain on paper towels.

Serve the falafel in warm pita bread with sliced cucumber, red onion, and tomato.

Add chopped mint and a dash of cayenne pepper to plain yogurt and serve it with the falafel.

# FISH-CAKE FLOUNDERS

With their crisp, bread-crumb coating, these are the ultimate fishy treat. You can serve them any way you like—and with a little creativity, you can make your own underwater scene.

## EQUIPMENT

- Cutting board
- Potato peeler • Sharp knife
- Saucepan • Dish towel
- Small bowl • Whisk or fork
- 3 shallow bowls or plates
- Potato masher • Wooden spoon • Skillet
- Spatula • Whisk or fork

## INGREDIENTS

- ¾ lb (340 g) Russet potatoes
- Small bunch parsley
- 3 x 5 oz (142 g) cans tuna in oil
- 2 small eggs
- ¼ cup (30 g) all-purpose flour
- ¼ cup (75 g) bread crumbs
- 2 tbsp butter
- Salt and freshly ground black pepper
- Vegetable oil, for frying

**1** Peel the potatoes, cut them into large chunks, and place in a saucepan of salted water. Bring to a boil and cook for 15–18 minutes, until tender.

**2** Meanwhile, wash and dry the parsley, cut off the stems, and finely chop the rest. Drain off any liquid from the tuna fish.

**3** Beat the eggs with the whisk or fork in the small bowl. Put the eggs, flour, and bread crumbs into the 3 separate shallow bowls or plates.

**4** When the potatoes have cooked, drain off the water and mash them in the pan. Stir in the butter and season with salt and pepper.

**5** Add the tuna fish and the chopped parsley to the mashed potatoes, then stir the mixture together well.

**6** Split the tuna mixture into 8 portions. Roll each one into a ball with your hands, then flatten it into an oval fish cake.

**7** Turn each fish cake in the flour to coat it completely, then dip it first in the beaten egg and then in the bread crumbs.

**8** Heat the vegetable oil in the skillet over medium heat. Gently fry the fish cakes on each side until crisp and golden brown.

Using canned tuna is really easy, but you can substitute canned salmon, if you prefer.

Serve the fish cakes with ketchup.

Green beans steamed until tender look like deep-sea plants.

## Fun fish dish

Using green beans and slices of lemon, you can magically turn fish cakes into funny flounders.

Use slices of lemon as fish tails.

Make an eye out of a slice of green bean.

## EQUIPMENT

- Grater or food processor
- 2 shallow bowls
- Mixing bowl • Whisk or fork
- Cutting board
- Sharp knife • Skillet
- Spatula • Sharp knife

**Ketchup**

## INGREDIENTS

- 1½ cups (115 g) bread crumbs
- Salt and freshly ground black pepper
- 2 eggs
- 4 boneless, skinless chicken breasts
- 2 tbsp vegetable oil
- Ketchup, to serve
- Mayonnaise, to serve
- Fries, to serve (follow the cooking instructions on the package)

**Mayonnaise**

# CHICKEN NUGGETS

If you like eating chicken nuggets, then try out this tasty version at home. They're easy to make and go well with all kinds of dipping sauces and fries.

**1** Put the bread crumbs into the shallow bowl and season. Crack the eggs into the other shallow bowl and whisk.

**2** Flatten the chicken breasts with your hands, then carefully cut them into chunks about 1 in (2.5 cm) across.

**3** Dip the chicken pieces into the egg and turn them to coat on all sides. Then coat them in the bread crumbs.

**4** Heat the oil in the skillet over medium heat. Fry the nuggets for 10–15 minutes, until they are brown on all sides and fully cooked.

The eggs help the bread crumbs stick to the chicken, making the nuggets extra crispy.

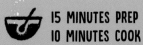

## EQUIPMENT

- Cutting board
- Sharp knife
- Grater or food processor
- Zester • Mixing bowl
- Whisk or fork
- 2 shallow bowls
- Frying pan • Spatula

## INGREDIENTS

- Small bunch parsley
- 1½ cups (115 g) bread crumbs
- 1 lemon to zest
- Salt and freshly ground black pepper
- 2 eggs
- 1 lb (450 g) skinned and boned white-fish fillets
- 1 tbsp vegetable oil
- 2 tbsp butter

# LEMONY FISH STICKS

Choose your favorite white fish for these crunchy and delicious fish sticks—it just needs to be boneless and skinless. Serve with wedges of juicy fresh lemon.

**1** Chop the parsley. Grate the zest from the lemon. Add the bread crumbs to the parsley and lemon zest in a mixing bowl and season.

**2** Gently whisk the eggs in the second shallow bowl. Cut the fish into fish sticks.

**3** Dip the pieces of fish in the beaten eggs and then in the bread crumbs. Make sure each fish stick is evenly coated.

**4** Heat the oil and butter in the skillet over medium-high heat. Fry the fish sticks for about 4 minutes on each side, until crisp and golden.

## EQUIPMENT

- Garlic press • Bowl
- Whisk or fork • Baking dish
- Baking sheet (if using a broiler)
- Tongs • Pastry brush
- Small saucepan
- Wooden spoon

## INGREDIENTS

- 12 pork spare ribs

### FOR THE BARBECUE SAUCE

- 1 garlic clove
- 2 tbsp dark brown sugar
- 2 tbsp light soy sauce
- 2 tbsp tomato paste
- 1 tbsp maple syrup or honey
- ½ tsp ready-made mustard
- Freshly ground black pepper

# BARBECUE SPARE RIBS

Sticky and sweet, these pork ribs are a fun and messy finger food that's great for a party or a summer barbecue feast. Just remember to hand out napkins!

**1** Crush the garlic. Put it in the bowl with the sugar, soy sauce, tomato paste, maple syrup, mustard, and pepper. Whisk well.

**2** Lay the ribs in the shallow dish. Pour the sauce over the ribs, then make sure they are all coated and leave to marinate for at least 20 minutes.

**3** Preheat the broiler or grill until hot. Broil or grill the ribs for about 15 minutes on each side. Brush with more marinade if needed.

**4** Heat any marinade that is left over in the saucepan, let it simmer, and serve it with the barbecued spare ribs.

Tomato paste

Each rib is coated with delicious barbecue sauce.

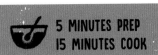
## EQUIPMENT

- Cutting board
- Skewers • Small bowl
- Pastry brush
- Baking sheet (if using a broiler)
- Tongs
- Metal skewer, for testing
- Sharp knife

## INGREDIENTS

- 20 cherry tomatoes
- 2 ears of corn, husks and silk removed
- Olive oil, for brushing
- Salt and freshly ground black pepper

# VEGETABLE BARBECUE

Grilling vegetables gives them a delicious sweetness. These veggies are great served on their own or with the ribs. You can grill other veg, too, such as bell peppers, zucchini, and onions.

**1** Preheat a grill pan over high heat or the broiler until hot. Thread the tomatoes onto skewers. Brush the corn with olive oil, then season.

**2** Broil or grill the tomatoes and ears of corn, carefully turning them so they cook evenly. The tomatoes will take about 5 minutes.

**3** When the corn is golden brown, push a skewer into it to see if it is tender. It should take 5–10 minutes to cook.

**4** Leave the cooked corn until it is cool enough to handle, then ask an adult to cut it into chunks about 1½ in (4 cm) wide.

Olive oil

Grilled corn

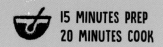
## EQUIPMENT

- Large saucepan
- Wooden spoon • Colander
- Cutting board
- Vegetable peeler
- Sharp knife • Grater
- Garlic press
- Large skillet or wok
- Plate
- Lemon squeezer

# CHICKEN CHOW-MEIN

A Chinese takeout favorite, this stir-fry is really easy to make at home. You can use different veggies, if you like. Just don't cook them for too long—they're delicious when they're crisp!

## INGREDIENTS

### FOR THE NOODLES

- 8 oz (225 g) soft chow-mein noodles
- 1 tsp sunflower oil

### FOR THE STIR-FRY

- 2 carrots
- 4 oz (115 g) French-cut green beans
- 4 oz (115 g) snow peas
- 4 scallions
- 1 in (2.5 cm) piece fresh ginger
- 1 garlic clove
- 2 tbsp sunflower oil
- ½ lb (300 g) skinless, boneless chicken breasts
- 1 tbsp soy sauce
- ½ lemon
- ½ tsp salt

Try using chopsticks to eat this meal.

Soy sauce

1. Half-fill the large saucepan with water and bring it to a boil. Add the noodles and boil them for 4 minutes.

2. Drain the noodles in the colander and rinse them in cold water. Return them to the pan and mix in the sunflower oil.

3. Peel the carrots and cut them into thin batons. Trim the beans and snow peas. Trim and slice the scallions.

4. Peel the ginger and grate it coarsely. Peel the garlic and either crush it with the garlic press or chop it finely.

5. Heat the oil in the skillet. Cut the chicken into strips, then stir-fry for a few minutes, until golden and cooked through. Put on a plate.

6. Heat the oil in the skillet over high heat. Add the garlic, ginger, carrots, and beans. Stir-fry for 4–5 minutes, turning regularly.

7. Add the chicken, snow peas, scallions, and noodles. Mix, then cook over medium-high heat for a few minutes more, stirring constantly.

8. Add the soy sauce, the juice of half a lemon, and the salt and mix once more. Cook for 2 minutes to heat through fully.

Chow-mein is noodles stir-fried with lots of tasty vegetables.

## Vegetarian chow-mein

For vegetarian chow-mein, replace the chicken with ¼ lb (115 g) zucchini and ¼ lb (115g) fresh or frozen broccoli.

## EQUIPMENT

- Cutting board
- Sharp knife • Grater
- Large skillet with lid
- Wooden spoon • Plate
- Saucepan with lid

## INGREDIENTS

### FOR THE CHICKEN CURRY

- 1 in (2.5 cm) cube fresh ginger
- 1 onion
- 2 cloves garlic
- 4 boneless, skinless chicken breasts
- 2 tbsp vegetable oil
- 1 tbsp mild Madras curry powder
- 1 cup (240 ml) chicken stock
- Salt and pepper
- ¼ cup (60 ml) plain Greek yogurt
- 2 tbsp chopped cilantro

### FOR THE RICE

- 1 small onion, finely chopped
- 2 tbsp (30 g) butter
- 1 stick cinnamon
- 1 tsp ground turmeric
- 1 cup (225 g) long-grain rice
- Pinch of salt
- 2½ cups (600 ml) chicken or vegetable stock

# CHICKEN CURRY AND RICE

A classic combo and a family favorite, this creamy, warming chicken curry and turmeric-yellow rice is hard to beat. The spicing is mild, so it's a real crowd-pleaser.

## Making the chicken curry

**1** Using a sharp knife, cut the peel off the cube of fresh ginger, then grate the ginger on the coarsest part of the grater.

**2** Peel the onion and the garlic, then chop them both finely. Carefully cut the chicken into bite-size pieces.

**3** Heat the oil in the skillet over medium-high heat. When hot, add the chicken pieces and cook quickly on all sides until golden, then move them to the plate.

**4** Fry the onion and garlic in the skillet until they turn brown at the edges. Stir in the ginger and curry powder and cook for 1 minute.

**5** Add the chicken, then the stock. Put the lid on the pan and cook over low heat for about 20 minutes, until the chicken is cooked through.

**6** Let the curry cool for a few minutes, then season with salt and pepper. Stir in the yogurt. Stir in the chopped cilantro.

You only a need a little turmeric to turn your food a beautiful sunshine yellow.

Put the rice out on a warm serving plate and spoon the chicken curry next to it.

## Cooking the rice

⚠ **1** Melt the butter in the saucepan over medium heat, add the onion, and cook until transparent. Add the spices and cook for 1 minute.

⚠ **2** Add the rice and salt and stir well. Cook over low heat for a few minutes more, until the rice looks transparent.

⚠ **3** Pour in the stock. Put a lid to the pan and simmer for 15–20 minutes, until the rice is tender and has absorbed all the stock.

## EQUIPMENT

- Bamboo skewers
- Cutting board
- Sharp knife • Mixing bowl
- Garlic press • Grater
- Whisk • 3 shallow bowls
- Saucepan • Wooden spoon
- Grill pan

## INGREDIENTS

### FOR THE KEBABS

- 1 small pork cutlet
- 2 small boneless, skinless chicken breasts
- 12 large cooked, peeled shrimp

### FOR THE MARINADE

- 2 tbsp soy sauce
- 2 tbsp honey
- Juice of 1 lime
- A few drops Tabasco sauce
- 1 clove garlic
- ½ in (1 cm) cube fresh ginger

### FOR THE SATAY SAUCE

- ½ onion
- ½ in (1 cm) cube fresh ginger
- 1 clove garlic
- 1½ tbsp vegetable oil
- 1 tbsp soy sauce
- 3 tbsp water
- 1½ tbsp light brown sugar
- 5 tbsp peanut butter
- Juice of 1 lime

### FOR SERVING

- 1 lime, cut into wedges

# KEBABS WITH SATAY SAUCE

A marinade is a sauce that slowly soaks into food to give it a delicious flavor. In this recipe, the pork, chicken, and shrimp are marinated for half an hour. Make the peanut satay sauce while the marinade works its magic.

## Preparing the meat

⚠ **1** Soak the bamboo skewers in water for 30 minutes. Cut the pork into thin diagonal slices, then cut each slice into narrow strips about 1 in (2.5 cm) wide.

⚠ **2** Flatten the chicken breasts with your hands, then carefully cut them into strips about 1 in (2.5 cm) wide.

## Making the marinade

**1** Put the soy sauce, honey, lime juice, and Tabasco into the bowl. Peel and crush the garlic, peel and grate the ginger, and stir them in.

**2** Pour the marinade into the 3 shallow bowls. Put the pork, chicken, and shrimp into the 3 bowls, turn them, and leave to marinate for 30 minutes in the fridge.

*Serve the kebabs with wedges of fresh lime and a bowl of satay sauce.*

**Pork kebabs**

Cut into strips and threaded onto skewers, the meat cooks quickly and the marinade helps it stay really tender.

## Making the kebabs

⚠ **1** Preheat the grill pan over medium-high heat. Thread the shrimp onto skewers. Fold the pork and chicken strips and thread them onto separate skewers.

⚠ **2** Grill the pork and chicken for about 4 minutes on each side, until brown and cooked through. Grill the shrimp for about 1 minute on each side, until lightly charred.

**Chicken kebabs**

**Shrimp kebabs**

## Satay sauce for dipping

## Making the satay sauce

Peel the onion and chop it very finely. Peel the ginger and grate it coarsely, then peel and crush the garlic. Heat the oil in the saucepan over medium heat. Add the onion and cook gently until soft. Add the ginger and garlic and cook for a few minutes. Put the onion mixture, soy sauce, water, sugar, peanut butter, and lime juice in a bowl and whisk.

**Peanut butter**

## EQUIPMENT

- Cutting board • Vegetable peeler • Sharp knife
- 3 saucepans • Colander or sieve • Bowl • Dish towel
- Screw-top jar
- Salad bowl

## INGREDIENTS

### FOR THE SALAD

- 8 new potatoes or 1 large potato, peeled and cut into bite-sized chunks
- 4 oz (115 g) French-cut beans
- 3 eggs
- 9 oz (250 g) cherry tomatoes
- 1 romaine lettuce heart or 1 head of baby gem lettuce, chopped
- ½ small red onion
- 3 x 5 oz (142 g) cans tuna in spring water or brine, drained

### FOR THE DRESSING

- 3 tbsp olive oil
- 1 tbsp wine vinegar
- ½ tsp French mustard
- Salt and freshly ground black pepper

# TUNA SALAD

This salad, inspired by a French tuna salad called "Tuna Niçoise," is so colorful: a rainbow on a plate. It's an excellent option for lunchboxes, too.

**1** Boil the new potatoes (or large potato, if using) until tender, carefully drain, and leave to cool. Cut the new potatoes in half.

**2** Trim the beans, then cook them in a saucepan of boiling water for 5 minutes, until tender. Drain and rinse under cold tap water.

**3** Boil the eggs for 8 minutes, then put them in a bowl of cold water to cool. Peel the eggs and cut them into quarters.

**4** Slice the tomatoes in half. Rinse and drain the lettuce leaves and pat them dry. Thinly slice the red onion.

**5** Put the olive oil, vinegar, mustard, salt, and pepper into the jar. Screw on the lid and shake well to make the dressing.

**6** Place the lettuce, potatoes, tuna, tomatoes, red onion, beans, and eggs in the bowl. Drizzle the dressing over the salad.

Boiled egg

Arrange everything in a salad bowl and mix gently to combine.

Single serving

## Mouthwatering salad

To turn the salad into a meal, serve it with warm French bread. Pour any leftover salad dressing into a bowl and serve it separately.

Extra dressing

**Scallions**

# TABBOULEH

This Middle Eastern salad packs in lots of fresh herbs. Add chopped tomatoes, too, if you like. It's the perfect side dish to serve at a barbecue.

## EQUIPMENT

- Heatproof bowl
- 1 large bowl
- Cutting board
- Sharp knife • Dish towel
- Large sieve • Salad bowl
- Wooden spoon

## INGREDIENTS

- 1¼ cups (175 g) bulgur wheat
- ½ cucumber
- 4 scallions
- 2 oz (55 g) fresh parsley, about ¾ cup
- 1 oz (30 g) fresh mint leaves, about 5 tbsp
- 3 tbsp olive oil
- 3 tbsp lemon juice
- Salt and freshly ground black pepper

**1** Put the bulgur wheat in the heatproof bowl, cover it with boiling water, and leave to soak for 20 minutes, until the grains soften.

**2** Finely chop the cucumber. Trim the scallions and slice them finely. Rinse, dry, and finely chop the parsley and mint.

**3** Drain the bulgur wheat in a sieve over a bowl. Use clean hands to squeeze out as much extra water as you can.

**4** Put all the ingredients for the tabbouleh into the salad bowl. Mix everything together and season with salt and pepper.

**Cucumber**

*Garnish the tabbouleh with sprigs of mint and serve it with slices of lemon.*

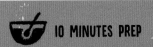
## EQUIPMENT

- Cutting board
- Sharp knife
- Four plates

## INGREDIENTS

- 1 extra-large ripe avocado
- 4 tomatoes
- 8 oz (250 g) buffalo mozzarella, drained
- Freshly ground black pepper
- 4 tbsp extra-virgin olive oil
- 6–8 fresh basil leaves
- Crusty bread, to serve

# TRICOLOR SALAD

This summery salad couldn't be simpler to put together. And the three colors of the ingredients match the colors of the Italian flag.

**1** Carefully cut the avocado in half. Remove the pit. Scoop the flesh onto a cutting board.

**2** Carefully slice the avocado, tomatoes, and mozzarella and arrange in overlapping slices on four plates.

**3** Season with the freshly ground black pepper and drizzle with the olive oil.

**4** Scatter the basil leaves over the salad and serve immediately with the crusty bread.

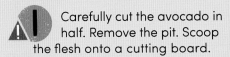
Crusty bread

Avocados are a creamy, mild-tasting fruit.

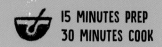
## EQUIPMENT

- Bowl • Whisk
- Ladle
- Small skillet
- Pastry brush
- Spatula
- Cutting board
- Grater • Sharp knife
- Wooden spoon • Spoon

## INGREDIENTS

### FOR THE CREPES

- ½ cup (65 g) all-purpose flour
- ⅓ cup (45 g) wholewheat flour
- Pinch of salt
- 2 eggs
- 1 cup (200 ml) milk
- ⅓ cup (100 ml) water
- 4 tbsp melted butter

### FOR THE MUSHROOM FILLING

- 8 oz (225 g) mushrooms
- 4 tbsp butter
- Pinch of grated nutmeg
- Salt and freshly ground black pepper
- 4 tablespoons heavy cream or sour cream

### FOR THE CHEESY FILLING

- 6 oz (175 g) Gruyère cheese
- 6 oz (175 g) smoked ham

# SAVORY CREPES

Turning crepes into a filling meal has never been easier. Pick one of these rich, savory fillings, go for both, or let your imagination run wild and come up with your own flavor combos!

Best served warm!

Mushroom crepe

## Making crepes

**1** Put both the flours and the salt in the bowl. Add the eggs and some of the milk and water, whisking them into the flour a bit at a time.

**2** Gradually pour the rest of the milk and water into the mixture, whisking until everything is evenly mixed.

**3** Add half the melted butter to the mixture and whisk it again to make the finished batter.

**4** Brush the skillet with melted butter and heat over high heat until it sizzles. Ladle in 2 tablespoons of crepe batter.

**5** Quickly tilt the pan from side to side, so that the bottom of the skillet is covered completely with a thin layer of batter.

**6** Cook the crepe for about 2 minutes, then flip it over using the spatula, and cook it for 30 seconds more. Slide it onto a warm plate. Repeat with the rest of the batter to make 12 crepes, brushing the skillet with more butter if needed.

Any mushrooms will work in this recipe: these closed-cup button ones are perfect.

These savoury crepes make a delicious light lunch or snack.

**Cheese and ham crepe**

## Mushroom filling

**1** Wipe and finely chop the mushrooms. Melt the butter in the skillet over medium-high heat and cook the mushrooms for a few minutes, until tender.

**2** Add the seasoning. Stir for a minute, then add the cream. Simmer for a few minutes until the filling is thick. Spoon a little filling onto a crepe and fold it over.

## Cheesy filling

Grate the cheese and dice the ham, then mix them together in a bowl. Sprinkle some of the mixture onto a warm crepe and fold it over.

51

*Fresh pesto*

## EQUIPMENT

- Saucepan • Colander
- Large, nonstick baking sheet • Sharp knife • Fork
- Mixing bowl
- Wooden spoon
- Rolling pin

## INGREDIENTS

- ½ lb (250 g) new potatoes
- 13 oz (320 g) frozen puff pastry sheet
- 1 cup (250 g) ricotta cheese
- 2 eggs, beaten
- 2 tbsp fresh pesto, plus extra for drizzling
- 2 tsp grated lemon zest
- ½ lb (225 g) cooked salmon, broken into pieces
- Salt and freshly ground black pepper

# SALMON, POTATO, AND PESTO TART

You can use puff pastry from a block. Roll out on a lightly floured surface to a rectangle measuring about 10 x 15 in (25 x 38 cm).

**1** Preheat the oven to 400°F (200°C). Scrub the new potatoes, then thinly slice each one.

**2** Boil the potatoes in a pan of lightly salted water for 5–6 minutes, until just tender. Drain and allow to cool slightly.

**3** Place the rolled-out puff pastry on a baking sheet. Using a sharp knife, score a 1-in (2.5-cm) rim along the sides of the rectangle, being careful not to cut all the way through. Prick the inside area lightly with a fork.

**4** In a bowl, beat together the ricotta cheese, eggs, pesto, and lemon zest with a wooden spoon, until well mixed. Season with a little salt and freshly ground black pepper. Stir in half of the salmon.

**5** Spoon the mixture inside the marked edge and scatter the potatoes and remaining salmon over the top. Bake in the center rack of the oven for 25 minutes, until the pastry is risen and the filling cooked.

**6** Remove from the oven and serve drizzled with extra pesto.

The rim left uncovered becomes tasty and crisp in the oven.

*Great party food!*

Ricotta cheese

## EQUIPMENT

- Skillet
- Wooden spoon
- Bowl • Fork • Grater
- Nonstick frying pan or grill pan • Sharp knife
- Cutting board

## INGREDIENTS

- 1 tbsp olive oil
- 1 sweet potato, peeled and cut into ½ in (1 cm) cubes (about 5½ oz/150 g)
- ½ x 14 oz (400 g) can black beans or kidney beans, drained
- 4 scallions, thinly sliced
- ⅓ cup (50 g) cooked corn, frozen or from a can
- 4 tbsp salsa
- Salt and freshly ground black pepper
- 2 large flour tortillas
- ½ cup (50 g) Cheddar cheese, grated
- Guacamole, to serve
- Salad, to serve

# SWEET POTATO AND BLACK BEAN QUESADILLA

You can't go wrong with toasted tortillas and melted cheese, especially when you add lots of Mexican flavors to the mix.

Guacamole

1. Heat the olive oil in the frying pan over medium heat, add the sweet potato, and cook for 6–8 minutes, stirring occasionally, until softened and lightly golden.

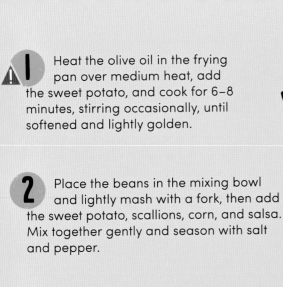

**Corn**

2. Place the beans in the mixing bowl and lightly mash with a fork, then add the sweet potato, scallions, corn, and salsa. Mix together gently and season with salt and pepper.

3. Spoon half the bean and vegetable mixture onto one half of one tortilla. Sprinkle half the grated cheese on top.

5. Wipe the cooled skillet with a paper towel, then heat it over medium-high heat. Place the tortillas in the pan and sear for about 2 minutes per side. The cheese should be melted and the outside golden-brown. Cut each quesadilla in half.

4. Repeat with the other tortilla, then fold them both in half to turn them into half-moon shapes.

6. Serve while they are warm, with guacamole and salad.

**Salsa**

Hearty and filling black beans can be replaced by any other cooked, canned bean or pulse.

**Black beans**

55

Tomato relish

# SPICY CHICKEN BURGERS

Coating the chicken for these burgers makes them extra tasty. Leave out the chili powder if you don't want the spicy heat, or use sweet smoked paprika instead.

## EQUIPMENT

- Cutting board
- Sharp knife • Plastic bag
- Skillet • Spatula
- Bread knife • Spoon

## INGREDIENTS

### FOR THE FILLING

- 2 large skinless, boneless chicken breasts
- ⅓ cup (50g) flour
- ¼ tsp chili powder
- Salt and freshly ground black pepper
- 1 tbsp vegetable oil, for frying

### FOR THE BUNS

- 4 sesame-seed hamburger buns
- Shredded lettuce
- Sour cream
- Spicy or mild salsa or sliced tomatoes

**1** Ask an adult to carefully cut the chicken breasts in half. Flatten them out by pressing them firmly with the palm of your hand.

**2** Put the flour, chili powder, a pinch each of salt and pepper, and the chicken in a plastic bag. Close the bag and shake it well.

**3** Heat the oil in the skillet until hot. Fry the chicken for 8 minutes on each side, until firm and golden brown and cooked through.

**4** Cut the buns in half. Fill each one with lettuce, a piece of chicken, sour cream, and salsa or sliced tomato.

### Nice spice

Chili powder and sour cream give these burgers a great Tex-Mex flavor.

# DELIGHTFUL
# DESSERTS

## EQUIPMENT

- Baking sheet • Sharp knife
- Saucepan • Sieve
- Parchment paper
- Wooden spoon
- Fork • 2 teaspoons
- Wire cooling rack • Bowl
- Whisk or electric mixer
- Serving plate

## INGREDIENTS

### FOR THE CREAM PUFFS

- Butter, for greasing
- 4 tbsp butter
- ½ cup water
- ½ cup (70 g) all-purpose flour
- 1 tsp sugar
- 2 eggs

### FOR THE SAUCE

- 4 oz (115 g) dark chocolate
- 2 tbsp butter
- 4 tbsp whipping cream

### FOR THE FILLING

- ⅔ cup (150 ml) whipping cream

# CREAM PUFFS

These light pastry puffs are such a treat, and they look impressive, too, if you pile them in a pyramid shape!

**1** Preheat the oven to 400°F (200°C). Grease the baking sheet and dampen it with water. Cut up the butter and heat it in the pan with the water on high heat.

**2** Sift the flour and sugar onto the wax paper. When the water boils, remove it from the heat and add the flour and sugar.

**3** Beat the mixture hard with a wooden spoon until it is smooth and comes away from the sides of the pan.

**4** Beat the eggs in the bowl, then beat them into the mixture, a little at a time, until you have a thick, smooth, glossy paste.

**5** Put teaspoons of the mixture on to the greased baking sheet, spaced out well. Bake for 20 to 25 minutes, until puffy and golden.

All-purpose flour

Eat the cream puffs as soon as you can, since they taste best when they're fresh.

**Chocolate feast!**

**6** Put the puffed baked pastries (choux buns) on a wire rack to cool. Pierce them with a fork to let out steam and keep them from going soft.

**7** Break the chocolate into a clean saucepan. Add the butter and cream. Stir over low heat until the chocolate has melted.

**8** Whisk the cream for the filling in the bowl until thick. Slice open each cream puff and fill with a teaspoon of cream.

**9** Arrange the cream puffs on the serving plate. Pour the chocolate sauce over the top, making sure each cream puff is lightly coated.

Use different types of chocolate for the sauce—white chocolate is yummy—or drizzle the cream puffs with salted caramel sauce.

## Chocolate éclairs

You can also use this recipe to make chocolate éclairs. Fill a piping bag with the cream puff mixture and pipe short fingers onto a baking sheet. Bake in the same way as the cream puffs. Fill with cream and top with chocolate sauce.

Sweet honey gives these a lovely rich flavor.

A lunchbox favorite!

## EQUIPMENT

- 12-hole muffin pan
- 12 paper muffin cups
- 2 small bowls • Large mixing bowl • Sieve • Wooden spoon • Fork • Teaspoon
- Wire rack

## INGREDIENTS

- 3 large ripe bananas
- 2 cups (275 g) all-purpose flour
- 2 tsp baking powder
- ½ cup (50 g) chopped pecans
- ½ tsp baking soda
- ⅓ cup (50 g) packed light brown sugar
- ½ tsp salt
- 1 large egg, beaten
- ¼ cup (100 ml) milk
- ¼ cup (100 ml) vegetable oil
- 5 tbsp honey
- 12 pecan halves

# BANANA, PECAN, AND HONEY MUFFINS

These fluffy, light muffins are perfect for breakfast or a midmorning snack, and they are a great way to use up ripe bananas.

**1** Preheat the oven to 375°F (190°C). Place the 12 muffin cups in the muffin pan. Peel the bananas, then mash them in a small bowl with a fork.

**2** In the large bowl, sift together the flour, baking powder, chopped pecans, and baking soda. Stir in the sugar and salt.

**3** In the second small bowl, whisk the egg, milk, oil, and honey with a fork. Add the bananas and mix well. Add the dry ingredients. Stir until just combined.

**4** Spoon the mixture into the muffin cases and top with a pecan half. Bake for 20–25 minutes, until risen and golden. Leave in the pan for a few minutes, then transfer to a wire rack.

Serve each parfait with a long-handled spoon.

# ICE-CREAM PARFAITS

Generous layers of sweet fruit, ice cream, and cream make these sundaes real summertime showstoppers.

## EQUIPMENT

- Cutting board
- Sharp knife
- Tall glass
- Spoon or ice-cream scoop
- Piping bag or spoon
- Long-handled spoon

## INGREDIENTS

### FOR THE STRAWBERRY PARFAIT

- ½ cup (55 g) strawberries
- 3 scoops strawberry ice cream
- Strawberry-flavored syrup
- 1 tbsp whipped cream
- 1 tbsp toasted, flaked almonds

### FOR THE BANANA-TOFFEE PARFAIT

- 1 ripe banana
- 3 scoops toffee or butterscotch ice cream
- Maple syrup
- 1 tbsp whipped cream
- 1 tbsp chopped pecan nuts or walnuts

**1** ⚠ Wipe the strawberries and remove the stems. Slice the fruit. If making a banoffee-toffee parfait, peel and slice the banana.

**2** Put layers of ice cream and sliced fruit in the tall glass. When the glass is nearly full, pour a little syrup over the top.

**3** Pipe or spoon whipped cream on top of the ice cream and fruit, then sprinkle with the nuts.

Keep the fruity vibes by using strawberry ice cream in your fruity parfait, or use vanilla instead.

**Banoffee parfait**

**Strawberry parfait**

# LEMON CHEESECAKE

This irresistible New York-style cheesecake is baked, then chilled and served cold. It's light and smooth, with zing from all the citrus and a delicious crunchy, buttery crust. Dessert delight!

## EQUIPMENT

- Plastic bag • Rolling pin
- Food processor • Plate
- Saucepan • Wooden spoon
- 8-in (20-cm) springform pan or round cake pan
- Zester or grater • Lemon squeezer • 2 large bowls
- Whisk or electric mixer
- Baking sheet • Metal spoon

## INGREDIENTS

### FOR THE CRUST

- 6 oz (175 g) graham crackers (for at least 2 cups of crumbs)
- 5 tbsp butter
- Butter, for greasing

### FOR THE FILLING

- 1 lemon
- 2 eggs
- 12 oz (340 g) cream cheese
- ½ cup (115 g) sour cream
- ½ cup (115 g) sugar
- 1 tbsp cornstarch

**1** Pulse the graham crackers in the food processor or seal them in the plastic bag and crush them using the rolling pin.

**2** Melt the butter in the saucepan over low heat. Turn off the heat and stir the graham cracker crumbs into the butter.

**3** Grease the cake pan. Pour in the cracker crumbs and press them down evenly to make a crust. Now make the filling.

**4** Peel or grate the zest from the lemon, saving some for the decoration. Cut the lemon and squeeze out the juice. Separate the white and egg yolks into two bowls.

**5** Wipe the food processor clean and use it to mix the zest and juice, egg yolks, cream cheese, sour cream, sugar, and cornstarch until smooth.

**6** Preheat the oven and baking sheet to 275°F (140°C). In the separate bowl, beat the egg whites with a handheld electric mixer until they form stiff peaks.

**7** Add the cheese mixture to the egg whites. Fold them in gently with the metal spoon until they are well combined.

**8** Spoon the filling into the crust and bake on the heated baking sheet for 40 minutes. Turn off the oven. Open the oven door and let stand for 10 minutes.

**9** Take the cheesecake out of the oven and cool. Remove it from the pan and put it on the plate. Chill it in the fridge overnight, if possible.

Sour cream gives the cheesecake mixture a refreshing tang.

Decorate the cheesecake with fine strips of lemon zest.

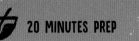

Lady fingers

## EQUIPMENT

- Grater or food processor
- Mixing bowl • Whisk
- Shallow dish • 4 individual glasses or 1 glass serving bowl
- Spoon • Teaspoon

## INGREDIENTS

- 2 oz (55 g) dark chocolate
- 1 cup (225 g) mascarpone
- 1 cup (225 g) fromage frais or ricotta
- ¼ cup (55 g) sugar
- 1¼ cups (300 ml) decaf coffee
- 20 sponge-cake ladyfingers

# TIRAMISU

A traditional Italian dish combining layers of silky and rich cream with coffee-soaked ladyfingers, this no-bake dessert is super quick to put together.

**1** Grate the chocolate with the grater or in a food processor. Whisk the mascarpone and fromage frais or ricotta and the sugar in a bowl.

**2** Pour the coffee into the shallow dish. Halve the ladyfingers, dip them in the coffee, and put a layer in each glass (or 1 large bowl).

**3** Cover the ladyfingers with a layer of the creamy mixture and sprinkle with a little of the grated chocolate.

**4** Repeat the layers, finishing with the creamy mixture. Sprinkle with grated chocolate. Chill in the fridge for 2 to 3 hours.

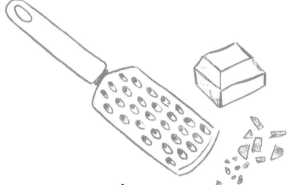

## Serving them in glass allows you to see the layers.

Chilling the tiramisu helps the flavors of the coffee, creamy cheeses, and chocolate to blend together.

Clafoutis is delicious when it has cooled a little but is still warm.

*Serve it with whipped cream!*

## EQUIPMENT

- 9 in (23 cm) round or square baking dish
- Cutting board
- Sharp knife • Saucepan
- Mixing bowl
- Wooden spoon or whisk
- Small sieve

## INGREDIENTS

- Butter, for greasing baking dish
- 1¼ lb (550 g) plums
- 3 tbsp butter
- 3 large eggs
- ½ cup (85 g) sugar
- ½ cup (100 ml) whipping cream
- ½ cup (85 g) all-purpose flour or almond meal
- Powdered sugar, for dusting

# CLAFOUTIS

This French baked pudding is usually made with black cherries, but plums are a great fruit swap.

**1** Preheat the oven to 375°F (190°C). Grease the baking dish. Cut the plums in half and remove the pits. Cut each plum half in two.

**2** Melt the butter in the pan. In the bowl, beat together the melted butter, eggs, sugar, cream, and flour or almond meal, until smooth.

**3** Pour the mixture into the baking dish and arrange the quartered plums in a pretty pattern on top of it.

**4** Cook the pudding in the oven for 40–45 minutes, until set in the center. Let it cool a little, then sprinkle with powdered sugar.

Plums

We use juicy and tangy plums here, but you can use chopped pears, apricots, rhubarb, prunes, or cherries instead.

# FRUIT CRUMBLE

There's nothing better than a comforting, fruity crumble on a cold day. This can be served with custard or vanilla ice cream.

## EQUIPMENT

- Baking dish • Cutting board
- Vegetable peeler
- Sharp knife • Saucepan
- Wooden spoon
- Mixing bowl • Spoon

## INGREDIENTS

### FOR THE FILLING

- Butter, for greasing
- 1½ lb (675 g) Granny Smith or other firm pie apples
- 3 tbsp brown sugar
- 1 tsp ground cinnamon
- 2 tbsp apple juice
- 8 oz (225 g) blackberries

### FOR THE CRUMBLE

- 8 tbsp butter
- 1⅓ cups (175 g) all-purpose or whole-wheat flour
- ¼ cup (55 g) rolled oats
- ½ cup (85 g) packed brown sugar
- ¼ tsp salt

**1** Preheat the oven to 375°F (190°C). Grease the baking dish. Peel the apples, cut them into quarters, cut out the cores, and then slice them.

**2** Cook the apples, sugar, cinnamon, and apple juice gently in the saucepan until the apples are soft, but not pulpy.

**3** Make the crumble mix: rub the butter and flour together in the mixing bowl until sandy, then mix in the oats, sugar, and salt.

**4** Put the apples into the baking dish and mix in the blackberries. Spread the crumble on top and bake for 25–30 minutes.

You can use chopped apricots, plums, or raspberries instead of blackberries in the crumble.

*Apple*

## EQUIPMENT

- Grater • Cutting board
- Sharp knife
- Large serving bowl

## INGREDIENTS

- 1 lb (450 g) fresh pineapple
- ½ a melon
- 9 oz (250 g) mixed seedless grapes
- 1 kiwi • 1 fresh mango
- ⅓ cup (100 ml) pineapple juice
- Grated zest and juice of 1 lime

*You can make fruit salad with any fruit you like.*

Mango

Kiwi

# FRUIT SALAD

Refreshing, colorful, and so easy, this salad is a perfect way to serve up your favorite fruit.

⚠ **1** Cut up the pineapple. Cut the melon into slices, remove the seeds and skin, then cut the slices into chunks. Cut the grapes in half.

⚠ **2** Peel the kiwi and halve it lengthwise, then thinly slice. Peel the mango, remove the core, cut it into chunks (see page 93).

**3** Put all the fruit in the bowl, pour the pineapple and lime juice on top, add the zest, and stir everything together.

## EQUIPMENT

- 1 heatproof bowl • 2 bowls
- Saucepan • Wooden spoon
- 4 ramekins
- Whisk or electric mixer
- Large glass bowl
(clean and grease-free)
- Large metal spoon

## INGREDIENTS

- 4 oz (115 g)
dark chocolate
- Butter, for greasing
- ¼ cup (55 g) sugar
- 5 medium eggs
- Pinch of salt
- Powdered sugar, for dusting

# HOT CHOCOLATE SOUFFLÉS

For everyone who loves chocolate, these fluffy little soufflés are a surefire hit. They are best served warm.

**1** Preheat the oven to 400°F (200°C). Break the chocolate into the heatproof bowl. Melt over a pan of simmering water, stirring until smooth.

**2** Remove the chocolate from the heat. Grease the ramekins lightly and sprinkle with a little of the sugar.

**3** Separate the eggs into two bowls. Stir the rest of the sugar and four of the egg yolks into the melted chocolate.

**4** Beat all five egg whites with a pinch of salt in the glass bowl until they form stiff peaks. Fold gently into the chocolate.

**5** Fill the ramekins until they are nearly full. Bake for 15 minutes, until the soufflés rise and puff up. Sprinkle with powdered sugar and serve.

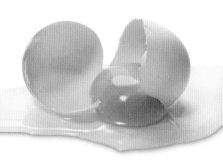

## EQUIPMENT

• 2 bowls • Fork • Whisk or electric mixer • Large metal spoon • 4 ramekins

## INGREDIENTS

• 10 oz (285 g) raspberries
• 1 tsp lemon juice
• 2 tbsp sugar
• ⅔ cup (150 ml) whipping cream
• ½ cup (140 ml) fromage frais or marscapone

# RASPBERRY FOOLS

This fruity, frothy, whipped-cream dessert couldn't be quicker to conjure up for a treat on a hot summer's day.

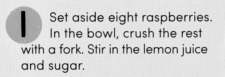

**1** Set aside eight raspberries. In the bowl, crush the rest with a fork. Stir in the lemon juice and sugar.

**2** Pour the whipping cream into the other bowl and beat it with the whisk or electric mixer until it has thickened.

**3** Using the large metal spoon, fold the fromage frais or mascarpone and whipped cream gently into the raspberries. Spoon the fool into the four ramekins.

## Try this

Try making the fool with other types of soft fruit, such as strawberries. Leave out the lemon juice and the sugar—the fruit may be sweet enough. Once you have made the fool, taste it and add sugar, if necessary.

*Keep the fools chilled until you are ready to serve them.*

Decorate the fools with the remaining whole raspberries.

## EQUIPMENT

- Large glass serving bowl
- Small saucepan
- Wooden spoon
- Large saucepan
- 2 bowls • Whisk or fork
- Cutting board
- Knife • Colander
- Electric mixer
- Palette knife

## INGREDIENTS

### FOR THE TRIFLE

- 8 oz (225 g) pound cake, cut into cubes
- 8 oz (250 g) fresh blueberries, plus extra to decorate
- 2 tbsp sugar
- 2 tbsp blackberry jam
- 6 oz (150 g) fresh strawberries, hulled and quartered
- 5 oz (125 g) fresh raspberries

### FOR THE CUSTARD

- 1¼ cups (300 ml) whipping cream
- 1 tbsp cornstarch
- 3 egg yolks
- ¼ tsp vanilla extract
- 2 tbsp sugar

### FOR THE TOPPING

- 1¼ cups (300 ml) whipping cream
- 2 tbsp sugar
- 2 tbsp toasted, flaked almonds

# TOTALLY TERRIFIC TRIFLE

A trifle is a layered dessert with cake, custard (or pudding), fruit, and whipped cream. You can change the ingredients based on the season and your tastes.

**1** Lay the cake cubes in the serving bowl. Place the blueberries in the small saucepan with the sugar, jam, and 1 tablespoon of water.

**2** Put the pan on low heat and stir until the sugar dissolves and the jam melts. Cook gently for 2–3 minutes, until the berries just burst; remove from the heat. Place in a bowl and chill.

**3** Put the cream for the custard in the large saucepan and heat gently until it almost boils. Whisk in the cornstarch, egg yolks, vanilla extract, sugar, and salt in a bowl.

**4** As soon as the cream boils, whisk it into the egg mixture a little at a time. Keep stirring the mixture to stop it from curdling.

**Custard**

You can use two 8 oz (237 ml) jars of chilled fresh custard if you don't want to make the custard from scratch.

**5** Return the mixture to the pan and stir it over very low heat until it thickens. Remove from the heat and leave to cool.

**6** Spoon the blueberries and juice over the cake in the bowl. Scatter the strawberries and raspberries on top, reserving a few for decoration.

*Tempting trifle!*

Creamy, fruity trifle is a good dessert for a party, summer barbecue, or other special occasions.

**7** When the custard has cooled completely, carefully spoon it over the layer of berries, making sure it is spread out evenly.

**8** Beat the cream for the topping using the electric mixer until it forms soft peaks, then spoon over the top of the trifle.

**9** Decorate with the reserved berries and sprinkle the toasted almonds on top. Serve immediately or chill in the fridge.

**Raspberry**

**Strawberry**

# CHOCOLATE BROWNIES

Gooey and moist, these brownies are sure to be a hit. Add chocolate chips or chopped nuts to the dough, if you like.

## EQUIPMENT

- 8 in (20 cm) square baking pan • Parchment paper
- Small saucepan • Wooden spoon • Large mixing bowl
- Whisk • Sieve • Rubber spatula • Toothpick
- Cutting board
- Sharp knife

## INGREDIENTS

- 11 tbsp unsalted butter, cut into cubes, plus extra for greasing
- 1 cup (100 g) cocoa powder
- 2 large eggs
- 1¼ cups (250 g) sugar
- 1 tsp vanilla extract
- Pinch of salt
- ½ cup (75 g) all-purpose flour

*Cocoa-licious!*

Store in an airtight container to keep them fresh—they can be frozen, too.

**1** Preheat the oven to 325°F (170°C). Lightly grease the 8-in (20-cm) square pan and line the bottom and sides with parchment paper.

**2** Place the butter and cocoa together in the small saucepan over low heat, stirring frequently until the butter has melted. Remove from the heat and leave to cool for 3–4 minutes.

**3** Meanwhile, in the large bowl, whisk together the eggs, sugar, vanilla, and salt for about 2 minutes until pale. Add the cocoa and butter mixture and stir to combine.

**4** Sift the flour over the mixture and, using a rubber spatula, mix thoroughly. Pour the mixture into the pan, level the top, and bake for 18–20 minutes, until just firm to the touch and a toothpick inserted in the middle comes out with moist crumbs. Cool in the pan, then place on the board and cut into 16 squares.

**All-purpose flour**

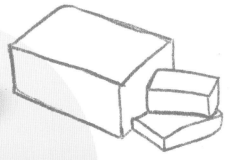

# TREATS AND SWEETS

**10 MINUTES PREP
20 MINUTES COOK**

**MAKES 12**

## EQUIPMENT

- 12-hole cupcake pan
- 12 paper cupcake cases
- Grater • Lemon juicer
- Measuring cup • 2 wooden spoons • Large mixing bowl
- Electric mixer • Sieve
- Wire rack • Mixing bowl
- Spoon

## INGREDIENTS

- 1 orange
- 12 tbsp butter, softened
- ¾ cup (175 g) sugar
- 1⅓ cups (175 g) self-rising flour
- 2 tsp ground mixed spice
- 2 large eggs
- 2 medium carrots, peeled and grated
- ½ cup (50 g) walnut pieces, chopped

### FOR THE FROSTING

- 8 tbsp butter, softened
- ½ cup (100 g) full-fat cream cheese
- 2 cups (240 g) powdered sugar, sifted
- 1 tsp orange juice

### FOR THE DECORATION

- Curls of carrot or edible decorations

# CARROT CUPCAKES

These mini carrot cakes, with rich cream-cheese frosting and warm spice, are the perfect snack.

**1** Preheat the oven to 350°F (180°C). Line the cupcake pan with the 12 paper cases. Grate the zest from the orange, then halve and squeeze the juice into the measuring cup. Set aside.

**2** Beat together the butter, sugar, and half the orange zest in the large bowl, using an electric mixer, until pale and fluffy.

**3** Sift in the flour and mixed spice, then add the eggs and orange juice. Whisk together until well combined.

**4** Stir in the carrots and nuts, then divide the mixture among the cupcake cases. Bake for 18 to 20 minutes, until risen and golden brown. Remove from the oven and place on the wire rack.

**5** For the frosting, beat the butter and cream cheese with the remaining orange rind, then beat in the powdered sugar a little at a time. Once all the powdered sugar has been added, beat in 1 teaspoon orange juice.

**6** Spoon the frosting on top of each cooled cupcake and decorate with carrot curls or your favorite cake decorations.

The orange and carrot make the cake extra moist.

**Grated carrot**

74

Orange decorations are perfect for these cakes.

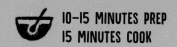 
## EQUIPMENT

- Baking sheet lined with parchment paper • 2 bowls
- Whisk or electric mixer
- Metal spoon • Wire cooling rack • Spatula
- Airtight container

## INGREDIENTS

- 2 medium eggs
- 1¾ cups (175 g) almond meal
- ¾ cup (175 g) sugar

# ALMOND COOKIES

These cookies, with their crackled tops and chewy, gooey centers, are hard to resist. For a fancy finish, dip the cooled cookies in melted chocolate, then leave to set.

*These cookies are very light and seem to melt in the mouth.*

**1** Preheat the oven to 350°F (180°C). Separate the egg whites from the yolks and put them in the 2 bowls.

**2** Put the yolks in the fridge, as you won't need them. Whisk the egg whites until they form stiff peaks.

**3** Add the almond meal and sugar to the egg whites and fold them in gently with the metal spoon until well mixed.

**4** Use damp hands to roll the mixture into about 22 walnut-sized balls, then put the balls on the baking sheet. Bake them for 15 minutes, until golden.

**5** Take the almond cookies out of the oven and cool them on a wire rack. Store them in an airtight container.

Almond meal

## EQUIPMENT

- Baking sheet lined with parchment paper • 2 bowls
- Heatproof bowl
- Saucepan • Wooden spoon
- Whisk or electric mixer
- Metal spoon • Wire cooling rack • Spatula
- Airtight container

## INGREDIENTS

- 2 large eggs
- 3 oz (85 g) dark chocolate
- 1¾ cups (175 g) almond meal
- ½ cup (115 g) sugar

# CHOCOLATE ALMOND COOKIES

Here's a sweet treat for chocolate-lovers. Make the balls as evenly sized as possible so they bake uniformly.

**1** Preheat the oven to 350°F (180°C). Separate the egg whites from the yolks. Put the yolks in the fridge, as you won't need them.

**2** Break the chocolate into the heatproof bowl and heat it over a pan of simmering water until melted. Stir until smooth. Remove the bowl from the pan.

**3** Beat the egg whites until they form stiff peaks, then fold the almond meal, sugar, and egg whites into the chocolate until mixed.

**4** Roll the mixture into 24 walnut-sized balls, then put the balls on the baking sheet. Bake for 15–20 minutes, then move to a wire rack to cool.

Once the cookies have cooled, store them in an airtight container to keep them tasting fresh.

## EQUIPMENT

- 9 x 9 in (22 x 22 cm) baking pan
- Large saucepan
- Wooden spoon • Metal spoon • Knife • Bowl
- Saucepan • Wire rack

## INGREDIENTS

### FOR PLAIN GRANOLA BARS

- 16 tbsp butter, for greasing
- 1 cup (225 g) butter
- ½ cup (85 g) sugar
- 2 tbsp maple syrup or honey
- 2 cups (340 g) rolled oats
- ¼ tsp salt

### FOR CHOCOLATE GRANOLA BARS

- 4 oz (115 g) dark chocolate

### FOR FRUIT-AND-NUT GRANOLA BARS

- 1 cup (115 g) raisins
- ½ cup (55 g) flaked almonds

# GRANOLA BARS

Buttery and rich, these yummy granola bars are both gooey and crunchy. And they're so simple to make. Keep them classic, or tweak them with fruits, nuts, and chocolate.

## Plain granola bars

**1** Preheat the oven to 350°F (180°C). Grease the baking pan. Place the butter, sugar, and maple syrup in the large pan and melt over low heat.

**2** Carefully take the pan off the heat. Add the oats and salt to the butter mixture and mix everything together well using the wooden spoon.

**3** Pour the mixture into the greased baking pan and press it down firmly using the metal spoon. Bake for 20–30 minutes, until golden brown.

**4** Cut the granola bars into squares and leave them to cool in the pan. Once they have completely cooled, take them out.

Fruit-and-nut granola bar

The longer you bake them, the crunchier they'll be.

Oats have a wonderful toasty flavor when they are baked.

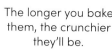

## Fruit-and-nut granola bars

**1** Make the plain granola bar recipe, but add the raisins and almonds to the mixture at the same time as the oats and salt.

Chocolate granola bar

## Chocolate granola bars

**1** Make plain granola bars and cut them into squares. Then break the chocolate into a heatproof bowl and stand it over a saucepan of water.

**⚠ 2** Heat the saucepan of water until it simmers. Stir the chocolate as it melts until it forms a smooth chocolate sauce.

**3** Dip one end of each piece of granola bar into the melted chocolate, then put it on a wire rack until the chocolate sets.

**Plain granola bar**

These can be cut and stored in an airtight pan, ready for snack time.

Raisins, almonds, and oats make fruit-and-nut granola bars an energy-filled snack.

## EQUIPMENT

- Large mixing bowl
- Electric mixer • Sieve
- Wooden spoon • 2 large baking sheets lined with parchment paper

## INGREDIENTS

- ⅔ cup (125 g) packed light brown sugar
- ⅔ cup (125 g) sugar
- 11 tbsp unsalted butter, softened
- 1 large egg, beaten
- 1 tsp vanilla extract
- 2 cups (250 g) all-purpose flour
- ½ tsp salt
- 1 tsp baking powder
- 6 oz (175 g) chocolate chips

*All-purpose flour*

# CHOCOLATE CHIP COOKIES

These cookies are crisp on the outside and chewy in the center. You can freeze the dough balls and bake the cookies from frozen—they will take about 2 minutes extra to bake.

**1** Beat together the sugars and butter in the mixing bowl with an electric mixer until smooth and creamy. Beat in the egg and vanilla. Sift in the flour, salt, and baking powder.

**2** Stir in the chocolate chips. Bring the dough together and roll it into 12 balls. Place 6 balls on each baking sheet, leaving space around each ball. Chill in the fridge for at least 1 hour.

**3** Preheat the oven to 350°F (180°C). Bake the cookies for 12–14 minutes, or until they are golden brown on the edges and slightly paler in the center.

**4** Remove from the oven and leave to cool on the baking sheets for 30 minutes before serving.

Swap the dark chocolate chips for milk chocolate chips, if you like.

If you don't have a piping bag, place widely spaced teaspoons of the cookie dough on the baking sheet instead.

## EQUIPMENT

• Grater • Baking sheet lined with parchment paper
• Mixing bowl • Wooden spoon • Piping bag with medium-sized star nozzle
• Wire cooling rack
• Heatproof bowl • Saucepan

## INGREDIENTS

• 16 tbsp butter, softened
• ½ cup (55 g) powdered sugar
• 1⅓ cups (175 g) all-purpose flour
• ½ cup (55 g) cornstarch
• ½ tsp vanilla extract
• Grated zest of 1 orange
• 6 oz (175 g) dark chocolate

# CHOCOLATE DIPS

Buttery, melt-in-the-mouth cookies and melted chocolate are a match made in heaven.

**1** Preheat the oven to 350°F (180°C). Using an electric mixer or whisk, cream the butter and sugar together in the mixing bowl.

**2** Add the flour, cornstarch, vanilla extract, and orange zest to the butter mixture and beat well with the spoon.

**3** Put the mixture in the piping bag and pipe it onto the baking sheet in 3-in (7.5-cm) lines. Bake for 15 minutes, until pale golden.

**4** Cool the cookies on the cooling rack. Break the chocolate into the heatproof bowl and melt it over a pan of simmering water.

**5** Carefully dip one end of each cookie into the melted chocolate and lay it back on the wire rack until the chocolate has set.

Substitute white chocolate for the dark, if you like, or melt both and have a mix!

Melt the chocolate until glossy and smooth.

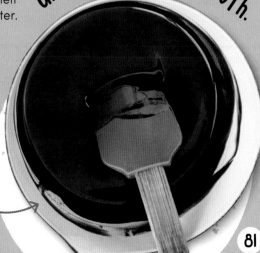

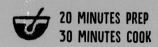

# RASPBERRY MUFFINS

Bake these muffins for a party—the fruit adds a yummy tang to the rich buttery sponge cake, and the chocolate chips are an extra treat! Use frozen raspberries if you can't find fresh.

## EQUIPMENT

- 12 paper muffin cups
- 12-hole muffin pan
- Saucepan • Sieve • Bowl
- Mixing bowl • Whisk or fork
- Wooden spoon
- Large metal spoon
- Spoon • Wire rack

## INGREDIENTS

- 8 tbsp unsalted butter
- 2 cups (285 g) flour
- 1 tsp salt
- 1 tbsp baking powder
- 2 eggs
- ½ cup (85 g) sugar
- 1 cup (220 ml) milk
- 8 oz (225 g) raspberries
- 3 oz (85 g) white chocolate chips

**1** Preheat the oven to 400°F (200°C). Put paper muffin cups in the muffin pan. Melt the butter in the pan. Sift the flour, salt, and baking powder into the bowl.

**2** Beat the eggs in the mixing bowl, then beat in the sugar, milk, and melted butter. Add the flour mixture and fold it in.

**3** Fold the raspberries and chocolate chips gently into the muffin mixture, then spoon it into the muffin cups.

**4** Bake the muffins for 25–30 minutes, until they rise and are firm and brown. Put them on a wire rack to cool.

The finished muffins are light and fluffy.

82

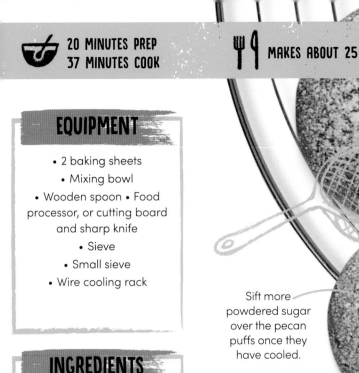

## EQUIPMENT

- 2 baking sheets
- Mixing bowl
- Wooden spoon • Food processor, or cutting board and sharp knife
- Sieve
- Small sieve
- Wire cooling rack

Sift more powdered sugar over the pecan puffs once they have cooled.

## INGREDIENTS

- Butter, for greasing
- 8 tbsp butter, softened
- 2 tbsp sugar
- 1¼ cups (140 g) pecans or walnuts
- 1 cup plus 1 tbsp (140 g) all-purpose flour
- ¼ tsp vanilla extract
- Powdered sugar for dusting

Vanilla extract

Pecan nuts

# PECAN PUFFS

These nutty little cakes are a bit like cookies, but are also light and puffy. Walnuts are a great substitute if you don't have pecans. Or why not try almonds or hazelnuts?

**1** Grease the baking sheets. Beat the butter in the bowl until soft, then beat in the sugar until creamy.

**2** Chop the nuts very finely, or grind them in the food processor until they are like fine bread crumbs.

**3** Preheat the oven to 300°F (150°C). Stir the nuts into the butter and sugar, sift in the flour, add the vanilla extract, and mix into a soft dough.

**4** Roll the dough into balls about the size of walnuts (about 25 balls) and put them on the baking sheets. Bake for 35 minutes, until golden.

**5** Sift powdered sugar over the puffs and put them back in the oven for 2 minutes. Place them on the wire rack to cool.

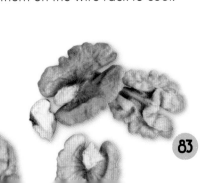

83

Flaked almonds

## EQUIPMENT

- 2 baking sheets lined with parchment paper
- Cutting board
- Sharp knife • Saucepan
- Wooden spoon
- Teaspoon • Wire cooling rack • Palette knife
- Spatula

## INGREDIENTS

- ¼ cup (55 g) flaked almonds
- ¼ cup (55 g) candied cherries
- 4 tbsp butter
- ¼ cup (55 g) sugar
- ¼ cup (55 g) candied lemon or orange peel, chopped
- 2 tbsp heavy cream
- 2 tbsp all-purpose flour
- 4 oz (115 g) semisweet chocolate

# FLORENTINES

A florentine is a type of chewy cookie made with fruits and nuts. They make a lovely gift at Christmas, packaged in pretty bags.

**1** Preheat the oven to 350°F (180°C). Chop the nuts and cherries finely. Melt the butter in the saucepan, then add the sugar.

**2** When the sugar dissolves, boil the mixture for 1 minute. Take the pan off the heat. Mix in the nuts, cherries, candied peel, cream, and flour. Put dollops of the mixture (spaced well apart) on the lined baking sheets.

**3** Flatten the dough a little with the back of a spoon. Bake the first sheet on the middle rack of the oven for 9–10 minutes, until the cookies have spread and the edges are golden brown.

**4** Remove the baking sheets and use a cookie cutter to form the round cookie shape. Return to the oven for 1–2 minutes, until the surface is a deep golden brown.

**5** Remove from the oven and leave the florentines on the baking sheet for 2 minutes, then remove to the wire rack, using a palette knife. Repeat with the remaining cookies.

**6** Melt the chocolate in the heatproof bowl over a pan of simmering water. Use the spatula to spread the chocolate on the back of each florentine.

Candied peel

Candied cherries

## EQUIPMENT

- Large heatproof bowl
- Large saucepan
- Wooden spoon
- Teaspoon
- 12 paper muffin cups
- Baking sheet
- Airtight container

The chocolate crispies take about 1 hour to set.

*Serve plain or top with sprinkles, chocolate eggs, or mini marshmallows.*

## INGREDIENTS

- 8 oz (225 g) milk chocolate
- 3 cups (85 g) corn flakes or puffed rice cereal

# CHOCOLATE CRISPIES

A party favorite, this no-bake recipe is so simple. You can experiment with different cereals and chocolates—let your imagination run wild!

**1** Melt the chocolate in the heatproof bowl over a pan of simmering water. Stir the chocolate from time to time until it is smooth.

**2** Add the corn flakes or puffed rice cereal to the melted chocolate and stir until the cereal and chocolate are evenly mixed.

**3** Spoon the mixture into the paper cases. Stand them on a baking sheet and leave in a cool place until the chocolate sets.

*Corn flakes*

Store the crispies in an airtight container to keep them fresh.

## EQUIPMENT

- Mixing bowl
- Wooden spoon
- 3 plates or shallow bowls
- Paper candy cups

## INGREDIENTS

### FOR THE TRUFFLES

- 2 oz (55 g) cream cheese
- ½ cup (55 g) chopped nuts
- ½ cup (55 g) powdered sugar
- ⅓ cup (30 g) cocoa powder

### FOR THE COATING

- Shredded coconut
- Cocoa powder
- Chocolate sprinkles

# CHOCOLATE TRUFFLES

These make a great gift—box them up with a ribbon for friends and family at Christmas! You can use any chopped nuts you like.

**1** Put the cream cheese, nuts, powdered sugar, and cocoa powder in the bowl and mix well. Roll the mixture into 16 small balls.

**2** Place the coconut on one of the plates, put the cocoa powder on the other plate, and pour the chocolate sprinkles onto the last plate.

**3** Roll the truffles in the cocoa powder, coconut, or sprinkles to coat them. Put the truffles in the paper candy cases.

Chocolate truffle coated in cocoa powder

Chocolate truffle coated in chocolate sprinkles

Chocolate truffle coated in shredded coconut

When the candies have set, put them in paper candy cases.

## EQUIPMENT

- Baking sheet lined with parchment paper
- Cutting board and sharp knife, or food processor
- Heatproof bowl
- Saucepan
- Wooden spoon
- Paper candy cups

## INGREDIENTS

- ½ cup (85 g) dried apricots
- ½ cup (75 g) blanched almonds
- ½ cup (55 g) raisins
- ¾ cup (140 g) white chocolate chips
- ½ cup (55 g) shredded coconut

*These candies make a good treat after a meal.*

Keep the candies in a cool place so they don't melt.

# FRUIT–AND–NUT BALLS

The possibilities are endless with these easy-peasy sweet candies. Try different dried fruits and nuts to create tasty snacks for you and your friends.

**1** Pulse the apricots, almonds, and raisins very finely in the food processor or chop them finely with a sharp knife.

**2** Melt the chocolate in the bowl over a saucepan of simmering water. Turn down the heat, then carefully stir in the chopped fruit, almonds, and coconut.

**3** Once the mixture has cooled down to hand temperature, roll the mixture into about 18 small balls. Put the balls on the baking sheet and leave them to set for 1–2 hours.

_Peanut butter_

# PEANUT BUTTER BITES

A bit like fudge, with a yummy layer of chocolate, but so much easier, these no-bake treats will disappear in no time.

## EQUIPMENT

- Saucepan • Mixing bowl
- Wooden spoon
- 9 in (22 cm) square baking pan
- Palette knife • Heatproof bowl • Knife

## INGREDIENTS

### FOR THE BITES
- 4 tbsp butter
- ¼ cup packed (55 g) dark brown sugar
- 1 cup (240 g) smooth, all-natural peanut butter
- 1⅔ cups (200 g) powdered sugar

### FOR THE TOPPING
- 6 oz (175 g) semisweet chocolate or chocolate chips
- 1 tbsp unsalted butter

**1** Melt the butter for the bites in the saucepan. Mix it in the bowl with the brown sugar, peanut butter, and powdered sugar.

**2** Spoon the mixture into the baking pan and spread it out evenly. Press it down firmly on top with the palette knife.

**3** Break the chocolate into the heatproof bowl (unless you are using chips), add the butter, and melt over a pan of simmering water.

**4** Spread the chocolate over the peanut butter mixture. Leave it to chill in the fridge until it has set but is still soft enough to cut.

**5** Cut the treats into 36 small squares and remove them from the baking pan, then put them in the fridge to finish setting.

Keep the peanut butter bites in the fridge until you are ready to eat them.

_Chocolate chips_

Peanut butter bites are good served at a birthday party.

## EQUIPMENT

- Mixing bowl • Whisk
- Sieve • Wooden spoon
- Cutting board • Baking sheet lined with parchment paper • Fork
- Bowl • Heatproof bowl
- Saucepan

## INGREDIENTS

- 1 egg white
- 2¾ cups (340 g) powdered sugar
- ⅛ tsp of peppermint extract
- A few drops each of red, green, orange, and yellow liquid food coloring (optional)
- 1½ oz (45 g) semisweet chocolate

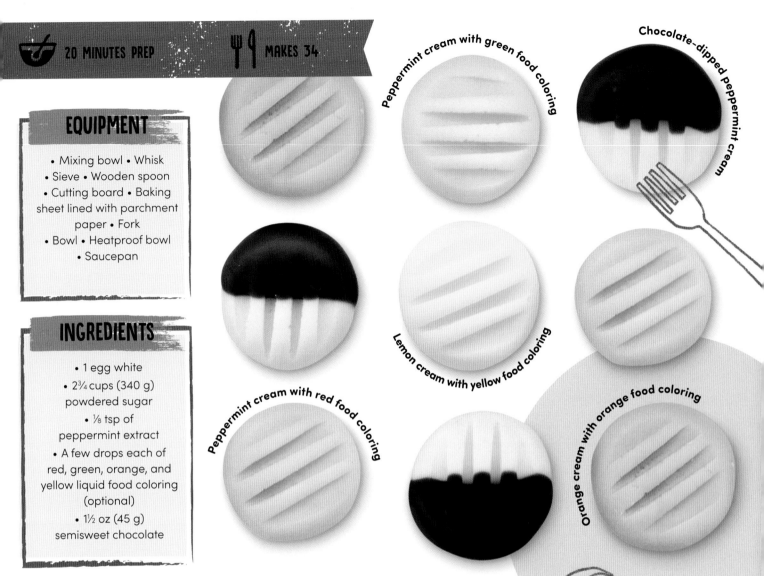

Peppermint cream with green food coloring

Chocolate-dipped peppermint cream

Lemon cream with yellow food coloring

Peppermint cream with red food coloring

Orange cream with orange food coloring

# PEPPERMINT CREAMS

Go easy on the peppermint extract the first time you make these—it's a strong flavor! Just like the treats on the previous page, they make for really cute gifts.

**1** Whisk the egg white lightly in the mixing bowl, until it is frothy but not stiff. Stir in 2 teaspoons of water.

**2** Sift the powdered sugar into the bowl, then stir it into the egg white with a wooden spoon until the mixture is stiff.

**3** Mix the peppermint extract into the dough. Divide the mixture into three balls. On a cutting board, knead food coloring into two of them, if using.

**4** Roll the mixture into small balls and put on the baking sheet. Flatten them with a fork, then leave to set for 24 hours.

**5** Break the chocolate and melt in a heatproof bowl over a pan of simmering water. Turn off the heat. Carefully dip some of the set peppermint creams into the chocolate.

Egg white

# CHEF'S KNOW-HOW

Follow these cooking techniques for making the delicious recipes in this book. Always ask an adult if you're unsure about anything.

## ⚠️ BROILING

To broil food, cook it quickly at a high temperature under a broiler. It is best to preheat the broiler before cooking the food.

## ⚠️ BAKING

Baking means cooking food in an oven. Turn on the oven in advance so that it is at the right temperature when you start baking.

## SEASONING

To season food, add salt, pepper, spices, or herbs to it. This gives it extra flavor. Taste the food to check if it has enough seasoning.

## ⚠️ FRYING

Frying means cooking food in a shallow layer of hot fat or oil until it is crisp and golden. Food is usually fried in a frying pan or skillet.

## ⚠️ SIMMERING

Simmering means cooking the ingredients over low heat on the stovetop so that the liquid is just bubbling.

## MARINATING

Marinating means soaking food in a sauce called a marinade before cooking. A marinade adds flavor and makes the food more tender.

## ⚠️ STIR-FRYING

To stir-fry food, cook it in a wok or large frying pan with a little oil. Cook it over high heat and stir it all the time.

## ⚠️ BOILING

Boiling means cooking the ingredients over high heat on the stovetop so that the liquid bubbles fiercely.

## DICING

**1** Dicing means cutting food into small cubes. To dice a vegetable, cut it in half lengthwise, then cut it into narrow strips.

**2** Hold the strips together firmly and slice across them, making small cubes. Move your fingers back carefully as you cut.

## SHREDDING LETTUCE

Hold the head of lettuce down on a cutting board and cut across it in fine slices. This will give you thin ribbons of lettuce.

## CHOPPING AN ONION

**1** Peel the papery skin off the onion. Leaving the root on will help to hold the onion together when you slice it.

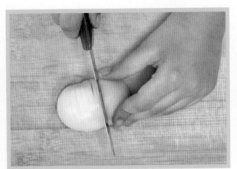

**2** Cut the onion in half through the root. Lay one half cut-side down and slice downward using a sharp knife.

**3** When you have cut the onion in slices one way, turn the onion and cut across the first slices at right angles.

## CHOPPING HERBS

To chop fresh herbs, bunch the stems together and hold them down on a cutting board, then slice across the leaves very finely.

## SLICING

To slice vegetables, hold them firmly on a cutting board and slice downward. Hold the knife against your knuckles, as shown.

## PREPARING FRESH GINGER

Cut the woody skin off the piece of fresh ginger. Slice the ginger finely. Cut the slices into thin strips, then cut the strips into small cubes.

## PITTING FRUIT

**1** Cut the fruit in half, following the crease down its side. Then twist each half of the fruit to loosen it from the pit.

**2** The halves of the fruit will come apart, leaving one half with the pit. Scoop out the pit using a small spoon.

## WHISKING

To whisk something means to stir it hard. Whisk eggs with a fork or whisk until the yolks and whites are mixed together completely.

## CREAMING

**1** To cream butter and sugar together, cut up softened butter and mix it with the sugar in a bowl using a wooden spoon.

**2** Then beat the butter and sugar together hard until the mixture is pale and creamy and drops off the beaters easily.

## BEATING

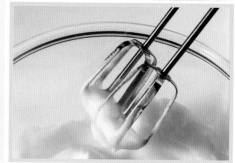

To beat egg whites, beat them lightly and quickly with an electric mixer until they are firm and stand up in little peaks.

## SEPARATING AN EGG

**1** Crack the egg near the middle by tapping it sharply against a bowl. Then break the egg open with your thumbs.

**2** Pour the yolk from one half of the shell to the other, so that the white slips into the bowl below. Put the yolk in a separate bowl.

## FOLDING IN

This is a gentle way of mixing two things together. Take scoops of the mixture and turn it over and around until it is mixed evenly.

## ROLLING OUT PASTRY

**1** Sprinkle the work surface and rolling pin lightly with flour. Flatten the ball of pastry with your hand, then roll it out away from you.

**2** Turn the pastry and roll it again, sprinkling it with flour if it sticks. Do this until the pastry is the shape and thickness needed.

## SIFTING

To sift flour or powdered sugar, shake it through the sieve. This gets rid of any lumps and makes the flour or sugar light and airy.

## RUBBING IN

Cut the butter into cubes, then rub it into the flour with your fingertips until the mixture looks like bread crumbs.

## ⚠ PREPARING A MANGO

Slice off the sides of the mango. Score a crisscross pattern on the mango flesh, then turn it inside out to create a hedgehog shape. Cut off the chunks.

## ⚠ CORING AN APPLE

Push a corer into the apple over the stem, then push it down to the bottom. Gently pull the corer out of the apple again. It will contain a cylinder of apple, including the core and the seeds.

## LINING A BAKING PAN

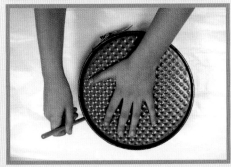

**1** Lay the cake pan on a piece of wax paper or parchment paper and draw around it. Then cut out the paper shape.

**2** Brush the inside of the pan with melted butter. Lay the paper inside. If it is wax paper, brush it with more butter.

## GREASING A PAN

Grease the baking pan or ovenproof dish by rubbing it lightly with butter, oil, or margarine. This stops any food from sticking to it.

# INDEX

**Senior Editor** Carrie Love
**US Senior Editor** Shannon Beatty
**Editor** Niharika Prabhakar
**US Editor** Margaret Parrish
**Senior Art Editors** Charlotte Bull, Kanika Kalra
**Art Editor** Bhagyashree Nayak
**Assistant Art Editor** Nishtha Gupta
**Jacket Designers** Rachael Prokic, Dheeraj Arora
**DTP Designers** Dheeraj Singh, Syed Md Farhan, Sachin Gupta
**Assistant Picture Researcher** Mayank Choudhary
**Production Editor** Nikoleta Parasaki
**Senior Production Controller** Ena Matagic
**Managing Editors** Penny Smith, Monica Saigal
**Managing Art Editor** Ivy Sengupta
**Delhi Creative Heads** Glenda Fernandes, Malavika Talukdar
**Deputy Art Director** Mabel Chan
**Publishing Director** Sarah Larter

**Illustrator** Rachael Prokic
**Recipe Editor** Laura Nickoll
**US Recipe Consultant** Renee Wilmeth
**Photography** Ruth Jenkinson, Amanda Haywood, Clive Streeter, Norman Hollands, Dave King
**Additional recipe writing and food styling** Denise Smart
**Home Economists** Nicola Fowler, Emma Jane Frost, Emma Patmore

This American Edition, 2023
First American Edition, 1997
Published in the United States by DK Publishing
1745 Broadway, 20th Floor, New York, NY 10019

Copyright © 1997, 2023 Dorling Kindersley Limited
DK, a Division of Penguin Random House LLC
23 24 25 26 27 10 9 8 7 6 5 4 3
004–333807–April/2023

A catalog record for this book
is available from the Library of Congress.
ISBN: 978-0-7440-7398-0

DK books are available at special discounts when purchased in bulk for sales promotions, premiums, fund-raising, or educational use. For details, contact:
DK Publishing Special Markets,
1745 Broadway, 20th Floor, New York, NY 10019
SpecialSales@dk.com

Printed and bound in China

**For the curious**
**www.dk.com**

MIX
Paper | Supporting responsible forestry
FSC™ C018179

This book was made with Forest Stewardship Council™ certified paper—one small step in DK's commitment to a sustainable future.
**For more information go to www.dk.com/our-green-pledge**

## Acknowledgments
Dorling Kindersley would like to thank Caroline Bingham for proofreading, Anne Damerell for legal assistance, Radhika Haswani and Robin Moul for editorial support, Veronica Nath and Medha Choudhary for hand modelling, and Helen Peters for indexing the revised edition of this book. Dorling Kindersley would also like to thank the original staff who worked on this title: Rachel Harrison, Mary Atkinson (Editors). Mary Sandberg, Claire Penny (Art Editors). Michelle Baxter, Susan Calver, Karen Chapman, and Helen Melville (Additional design). Josie Alabaster (Production). Sheila Hanly (Senior Managing Editor). Jane Horne (Deputy Managing Art Editor). Almudena Díaz, Nicola Studdart (DTP Designers). Emma Price-Thomas, Rachel Wardley, and Sarah Phillips (Additional editorial help), Amanda Harrold, Nicola Harrold, Stacey Martin, Sarah Mendham, Natasha Payne, Sam Priddy, and David Watts (Hand modelling).